The End of a Community

The Destruction of the Jews
of Bamberg, Germany, 1938–1942

by

Karl H. Mistele

Translated by
Jacob Feuchtwanger

KTAV Publishing House, Inc.
Hoboken, New Jersey

Copyright © 1995
The Ashe Foundation, Inc.

Library of Congress Cataloging-in-Publication Data

Mistele, Karl–Heinz.
    [Ende Einer Gemeinde. English]
    The end of a community : the destruction of the Jews of Bamberg, Germany,
1938–1942 / Karl H. Mistele.
        p.   cm.
    Includes bibliographical references.
    ISBN 0–88125-551–3
    1. Jews—Persecutions—Germany—Bamberg. 2. Holocaust, Jewish
(1939–1945)—Germany—Bamberg. 3. Bamberg (Germany)—Ethnic relations.
I. Title
DS135.G4B36513 1995
943'.318004924—dc20   95–30361
                                                                    CIP

The End of a Community was originally published in German in 1988 by the City Archive of Bamberg. We are grateful to the City of Bamberg for permission to translate it.

We gratefully acknowledge the cooperation of the Leo Baeck Institute in preparing the translation.

Publication of this volume was made possible by a grant from the Ashe Foundation, Inc., Stamford, Connecticut.

Manufactured in the United States of America
KTAV Publishing House, 900 Jefferson Street, Hoboken NJ, 07030

In memory of

Ilsa Ashe

1916 – 1995

Contents

Foreword to the English Edition

THE FOREWORD BY THE DIRECTOR of the Bamberg Municipal Archive and the preface by the author of this work were addressed to German readers. Some background information may be helpful for English-speaking readers.

Histories of the more important Jewish communities in Germany, written by rabbis and other scholars, have been available since the last half of the nineteenth century and Bamberg is no exception.[1]

In many instances, post–World War II accounts, bringing the histories up to date, have also appeared. In addition, local historical societies and individuals, both professional historians and amateurs, have published accounts of many of the smallest communities, usually under official village, town, or city auspices.[2] These generally include brief accounts of the Nazi period, particularly the pogrom in November, 1938 and the Holocaust. They provide information on the suffering of the

---

1 A. Eckstein, *History of the Jews in the Former Prince Bishopric of Bamberg* [Ger.] (Bamberg, 1899; reprinted 1984), ends in 1802. A. Eckstein, *Festchrift on the Occasion of the Opening of the New Synagogue in Bamberg* [Ger.] (Bamberg 1910; reprinted, 1985), takes up the history in 1802 and continues to 1861, when the numerus clausus system was discontinued in Bavaria.
2 See the annual bibliographies in the *Yearbook of the Leo Baeck Institute*.

Jews and often give lists of the doomed, as well as eyewitness narratives of the night of terror and the manner of the deportations, but few attempts have been made to deal exhaustively with the surviving documentation, or to relate local events to general policies applied throughout Germany.

The author of *The End of a Community*, the late Dr. Karl Heinz Mistele, was senior archivist at the Bavarian State Archive in Bamberg. Even before he embarked on this work in 1980, a part of Dr. Mistele's considerable learned output (amounting to 3,000 printed pages) had been concerned with aspects of the history of Jewish life in Bamberg and the surrounding country. The principal difficulty faced by Mistele during his eight years of research for this volume was that the Bamberg *Gestapo* had burned many of its files in 1945 before the arrival of the American Army. An attempt was also made to destroy the papers of the Bamberg Nazi Party, housed in the cellar of its headquarters, formerly the home of the *Ressource,* a club founded by Jews around 1837. Fortunately, the attempt was only partly successful. Mistele effectively used the surviving papers, as well as other sources not specifically related to Jews, such as the records of Bamberg's municipal housing department. In addition, he discovered and was able to utilize a brief but invaluable communal chronicle kept by Dr. Martin Morgenroth, the secretary (and sometime president and vice-president) of the Bamberg Jewish Community from 1930 to 1939.

The End of a Community is probably unique in the vast literature of the Holocaust. The deportation of Germany's Jews has been described elsewhere, but this book provides a detailed account of the experiences of a group of Jews who continued living in their hometown during the four years from the pogrom of November 9–10, 1938 to the end of their community on September 10, 1942. Throughout the work, events are linked to Nazi government policies, with specific local details and official

deceptions identified so far as is possible. The materials provided by Mistele shed new light on a wide range of topics,
including the exclusion of Jewish children from the public
schools, the pogrom of Novermber 9–10, 1938 and its aftermath, the Dachau concentration camp, the increasingly circumscribed life of Germany's Jews during the early years of World
War II, and ultimately the deportations for "resettlement" in the
east.

At one point in his researches, Dr. Karl Mistele asked himself
whether he should go on "digging in the filth of the ever con-
tinuing laws and decrees" that inexorably increased the deprivation and misery of the Jews he was studying. He answered in
the affirmative, seeing it as his duty to show the depths to
which German officialdom, without even a residue of humanity,
was capable of descending. As this indicates, one of the most
profound lessons offered by Mistele's book is its narrative of
how the legal procedures and bureaucratic methods of a seemingly civilized society can be channeled for the most brutal and
evil of purposes.

Herbert Loebl
April 1995

Herbert Loebl, born 1923 in Bamberg, escaped to Britain in December 1938. An engineer, economic historian and retired industri-
alist, he lectures on the roots of the Holocaust and is engaged in
family research. He lives in Newcastle-upon-Tyne, England.

Introduction

ON DECEMBER 10, 1988, in an address in Bamberg to the 37th Congress of German Historians, Federal President Richard von Weizsäcker spoke of Germany's looking at itself in the mirror of history as an act that required real strength and posed a temptation to avert the eyes or even to denounce the reflection as a distorted image. This look into the mirror at the birth of Nazism and its unspeakable crimes released a deep sense of bewilderment, and what other reaction could there have been? He warned the historians to have the courage to face the truth, not least in view of the Historians' Debate, and left no doubt that Auschwitz happened in the name and at the hand of the German people. For just this reason, our youth, who are seeking their place as Germans in today's world, who want to understand themselves and the world, and who want to keep their history alive, need the help of cool-headed historians.

In view of this candid confession I welcome the publication of Karl H. Mistele's book, which joins the previous publications describing the fate of the Jews of Bamberg in the years 1930 to 1942 and records the end of a community. I am delighted by the growing number of young academicians researching the history of the Jewish people in the city and diocese of Bamberg and the surrounding districts of Franconia. This confirms the opinion of our President regarding the Nazi crimes as an anomalous event in history.

Furthermore, there is a widespread feeling among the older people in this town that our Jewish fellow citizens constituted an extremely important minority, not only in our economic life, but also in the cultural and social sphere. Due to their expulsion and extermination our town suffered a perceptible reduction in the quality of life. Despite many persecutions and dishonorable treatment during their nearly thousand-year presence in Bamberg and the surrounding provinces of Franconia, it was not rare to find demonstrations of growing respect and reverence for Jews emerging in the nineteenth century along with full emancipation. Some friendships developed. A few even survived the worst phase of Nazi persecution. This is manifested in the names of the many endowments given to our town by prominent and wealthy Jewish families and also in the memorial to Jewish casualties who gave their lives on the battlefields of the First World War.

Even today many of those names have a familiar ring in our city. Every true Bamberger feels enduring shame and deep sorrow that even those citizens did not escape the fate of their brothers in the so-called Greater German Reich. All this should be a wake-up call for our younger population to study the history, circumstances, and events of this genocide on a local level—on the doorsteps of their parents, grandparents, and great-grandparents, so to speak. They should study these events to rebuff the siren call of incorrigible and misguided ideologists of today or of the future.

Thus I hope this volume will find a wide readership, an open reception, and careful study. The synagogue at Urban and Herzog-Max Streets, destroyed by the brown mob during the pogrom of November 8–9 [1938; actually 9–10] was dedicated to the highest concepts and ideals of Judaism in our community. I hope this book will bring the realization of this aspiration—

for the good of our children and grandchildren—in times more peaceful and humane than our recent past.

Paul Röhner, Lord Mayor
Bamberg

Foreword

WITH THE PRESENTATION by Karl H. Mistele of the Jewish community of Bamberg during the Nazi period until its total destruction in 1942, the publications of our Municipal Archive take on a new dimension. The scientific methods of historians pale in comparison to the actual injustice and suffering of victims caught in the wheels of Nazi racial hate. "Words and pictures fail in the face of the Holocaust" (Prime Minister of Bavaria Max Streibl, Nuremberg, October 24, 1988).

The denial of civil rights to Jews and the refusal to allow them to participate in community affairs was visible to everyone. Knowledge of the Final Solution became common after the war. Nevertheless, it has a special impact in a local setting, where places, people, and circumstances are familiar and well known. Events so close at hand increased the perception of wrongs done, evoking shame in perpetrators and utter perplexity in those who would not or could not protest. In view of the opinion that Bamberg was less conformist and less captivated by Nazi ideology, it is hard to conceive that such excesses occurred. Lack of understanding of the state's power to force the population to comply and underestimation of human weakness lead us to overlook the possibility of a gradation of evil during the Nazi regime.

The Municipal Archive has decided to inform the public of all the brutal aspects of these calamitous times. The time has come for historians of this region to step up their research into the Nazi era. The dearth of information on its aspects in Bamberg is now eliminated.

The role of the Archive in this publication is not to take a stand in the dispute over collective guilt based on any academic, political, or legal viewpoint. Nor is it a forum for allocating blame or for discussing the abnormality of the Holocaust. Our only intention is to contribute to the prevention of a recurrence of an evil of such magnitude. This work is an act of historical justice to serve as a reminder and a warning.

Our thanks go to the author, who was able to address a delicate topic with well-grounded experience and with scientific reliability. His knowledge of source material and his expertise allowed us to publish a well-rounded description, notwithstanding the enormity of the accompanying documents. To him belongs the credit. He was the first to depict the facts in a true and clear light.

We hope his book will stimulate further research into the history of the Jews of Bamberg.

Robert Zink, Director
City Archives, Bamberg

Preface

The idea of writing about the end of the Jewish community of Bamberg originated in the fall of 1980, when I happened upon a copy of a Jewish identity card. What until then had been an abstract concept took on a human dimension. Faces appeared; people and their destiny materialized. History became an intense presence, a presence which cried out for explanation.

At times my self-imposed task was hard to carry out, when the lack of sources forced me into tortuous detours or when the language of the documents was too explicit. I feared that the task to "tell it as it is" would founder on my own failure to grasp the facts.

To achieve completeness in such an account is impossible. Yet this description, alas incomplete, speaks loud and clear.

My thanks go to all who assisted me, either in the search for sources or in their interpretation. Also, my gratitude to the city of Bamberg for publishing this dark chapter about our town in the series of publications by the Archive. And special thanks to my wife, who patiently, not only suffered through eight years of work on a dreadful subject, but, through her critical perception, helped greatly to bring this project to fruition.

Karl H. Mistele

1

The Jewish School System

ALTHOUGH THE MANIFESTATIONS OF JEW HATRED in Bamberg were less brutal than in Nuremberg, where the anti-Semitism was more obtrusive and more primitive, the city was no island of saints. Boycott Saturday in 1933 (April 1) showed this, as did the confiscation of the Ressource building, the center of Jewish social life. The Jews of Bamberg became nonpersons; acquaintances considered them nonentities, as signs posting the notice JEWS NOT WELCOME barred entry to shops, and formerly respected members of clubs and associations—notified by more or less politely worded communications—found themselves excluded. The expulsion of Jews from the city's social life, planned, controlled, and often welcomed, accelerated after the enactment of the Nuremberg Laws in September 1935. Jews were less often subject to brutal public outrages, for administrative measures offered more possibilities. Even so relatively harmless a matter as school administration was used as a tool for denigrating them. This is shown clearly by the ordinance of the Ministry of Education on April 1, 1936, establishing guidelines for segregated classes for Jewish pupils in public elementary schools.

Until then Jewish and "Aryan" pupils had attended the same classes and schools. According to the recollections of former students, "joint" education was never a problem. This may have been the case in the 1920s, but the presence of nationalistic and anti-Semitic teachers in Bamberg casts some doubt on the reports of harmonious and trouble-free coexistence. There was always a festering tension among the students, leading to taunts and quarrels.

A remark in the files of one student points to the difficulties that existed in the 1930s. A report by a teacher, dated April 2, 1936, describes a student at the Rupprecht School: "Jew, well-liked because of his quiet behavior and his willingness to help his classmates; enthusiastic and responds to encouragement; mother supportive and thankful for the fair treatment of the boy." The mother's gratitude for the fair treatment of her son is emphasized; did she have different experiences on other occasions?

Even if we assume that the reports of idyllic Christian-Jewish coexistence in the Bamberg school system, as seen through the eyes of contemporaries after 50 years, are true, a critical observer in those days could not have overlooked the facts which later led to a bitter end—the end that was heralded by an order of the Ministry of Science, Education and Culture of the Reich and Prussia, issued in August 1935, weeks before the proclamation of the Nuremberg Laws, to register the race of all children in public elementary schools. On September 19, a form was distributed to school administrators, advising them to segregate children of non-Aryan extraction. A certain urgency was evident, because a covering letter stated: "The registration is to be handled with utmost delicacy, but with deliberate speed to meet the deadline set by the responsible authorities."

All this was to be accomplished with the cooperation of the victims.

> No proof of descent is required at this time. It will be sufficient to record the declarations of parents or guardians as submitted to the teacher—either in writing or orally—that after careful investigation it can be stated with certainty that

no parent or grandparent was of non-Aryan descent or professed the Jewish religion. Parents or guardians who are not able to attest to the Aryan descent of the child will be required to assist the principal in filling out the form based on available information.

The seeds were planted for what became obvious during the completion of the Final Solution after 1941: the horrendous abuse of administrative procedures leading to the victims' assistance in their own destruction.

At this point it was only the segregation of Jewish children in elementary schools. On May 11, 1936 the Bamberg Board of Education reported to the government of Upper Franconia:

> Forty-five Jewish children are registered in elementary schools in Bamberg. This number is sufficient to require the opening of a Jewish elementary school. Negotiations are under way between the board of education and other city agencies on one side, and the representative of the Bamberg Jewish community, Attorney Dr. Morgenroth, on the other. Since the proclamation of Ordinance No. 1183 b a 1 of April 17, 1936, letters have been exchanged and face-to-face meetings have been held to facilitate the establishment of a segregated school. In Bamberg this requires only one classroom, and such a facility is hard to find.
>
> Without regard to the lack of space in Bamberg's schoolhouses—necessitating an ongoing expansion program—there cannot be, on principle, a Jewish school in a German schoolhouse.

An official memo from the chairman of the board of education, dated April 28, 1936, touched on this subject.

> . . . in principle it is absolutely impossible to house Jewish classes in a German schoolhouse. . . . All we need is the procurement of a schoolroom which will be supplied with used desks and blackboards. . . . Of course such a room must con-

form to hygienic requirements, as long as such Jewish classes are still under the jurisdiction of the public elementary school system, or at least until the enactment of an official Reich law. I have advised Attorney Morgenroth to search for a suitable room in a Jewish building, such as the old synagogue or the former White Dove Inn, for which the Bamberg municipality can pay the rent. . . . In this matter I ask for the support of the Lord Mayor, in order to have our schools *judenrein* [free of Jews] as soon as possible.

On April 17, 1936, the government in Ansbach sent an explicit letter to the Bamberg board and the rest of the district regarding "the segregation of Jewish children in elementary schools." It dispensed advice on how to make schools *judenrein.*

In places where *in spite of the existence of Jewish private or public schools,* Jewish children are attending Christian or general public schools, it is easy to avoid the establishment of a segregated Jewish school system by requiring Jewish parents and guardians to enroll the children in the existing Jewish schools. This has been done in Nuremberg with great success. [Emphasis in original document].

What kind of "emphatic advice" was given to the Jewish parents in Nuremberg? Even before the official enactment of the national law, the expulsion of Jewish children from public schools achieved the hoped-for results. Finally, the Jewish community reluctantly offered to open the Jewish school in the conference room of the synagogue at Herzog-Max St. 13. On October 6, 1936, the directors of the community sent a letter to the Lord Mayor:

As an interim solution, but no more, we are willing to allow the city the use of the conference room for the Jewish elementary school, even though this will cause a shortage of space for our own purposes. Also, the use of a single room—

not particularly large—and without adjoining rooms, does not provide a satisfactory environment for teaching.

Everything proceeded according to the well-oiled machinery of government offices. An agreement was reached on the rent for the classroom: 150 marks, payable by the city of Bamberg. The hiring of teachers and the drafting of their contract proceeded with the punctilious exactitude of government bureaucracy. The list of applicants for a teaching position at the newly established Special School for Jewish Children survives. The applicants were:

1. Dr. Stefan Bielschowski, teacher at a secondary school in Charlottenburg. Born 1895. The answer to the question "Summary of Reasons for Application" read: "Certificate of Matriculation from Gymnasium; 8 semesters of courses in philosophy and French; license to teach mathematics, French, and Latin in secondary schools. Received degree in Prague."
2. Justin Frankel, teacher at the Jewish elementary school, instructor of religion and cantor in Erlangen. Born 1896. Reason for application: diminishing school population in Erlangen.
3. Leo Eland, clergyman. Elementary school teacher and religious instructor in Zittau. Born 1896.
4. Walter Riesenfeld, Caputh, near Potsdam, Born 1901, "Graduated Gymnasium; studied at university (biology, philosophy, etc.); Teachers' Seminary in Frankfurt/Main." Last position: teacher and tutor at boarding school in Caputh.

Justin Frankel was hired. The documents concerning his terms of employment make up a large part of the relevant file in the Ministry of Education:

. . . Starting salary of a permanent teacher in elementary schools, at present 2,800 reichmarks a year; housing allowance 606 reichmarks (Grade B). . . . Frankel, born 10/28/96, has two children. (Edith, born 4.XIX.27. and Ernst, born 10.XI.24). . . .

Classes at the Special Jewish School in Bamberg started on November 5, as a one-room elementary school.

The Reichsvertretung der Juden in Deutschland (Central Organization of Jews in Germany) and its education department had already given much thought to the curriculum of the segregated Jewish schools. An undated copy of its "Guidelines for the Creation of a Curriculum for Jewish Elementary Schools" points to the attempt to put the total exclusion of Jews from the German nation to good use in areas of education and instruction; a return to "true Jewishness"—something neglected, even denied, in wide circles of German Jewry.

The return to true Jewishness in Bamberg was in many cases not a top priority. A notice from the congregation's administration to parents of school-age children (unfortunately undated) suggested that it was not in the best Jewish interest to send children to school on holidays that exempted Jews from attendance. This practice represented an unfavorable picture to the gentile world, giving the impression of lack of respect by Jews for their sacred heritage.

Following are the guidelines for a curriculum in Jewish elementary schools:

Copy of No. IV 60672
Reichsvertretung der Juden in Deutschland
Department of Education

Guidelines for the Creation of a Curriculum
in Jewish Elementary Schools
(Revised Version)

Introduction

The purpose of the following guidelines is to create a framework for the educational and instructional objectives in Jewish elementary schools in Germany.

The assumption is that the curriculum of the Jewish schools has to conform to the standing regulations for all elementary schools, but also has to do justice to the special character of a Jewish school.

The guidelines are, first, a clarification of the overall objectives of a Jewish school; second, advice on the part of the curriculum that has a special impact on the administration of Jewish schools charged with these exceptional educational tasks.

Governmental regulations must be followed when creating a curriculum for Jewish schools.

General Objectives

The school must be imbued with a self-assured Jewish spirit. The maturing children should have a healthy confidence in their Jewishness. They should learn to find happiness in being a Jew, the pride as well as the deprivation that comes with it. To achieve these aims, Jewishness has to be the focal point in all suitable subjects. The objective is to arouse and nurture a real understanding of the perpetuity of the Jewish religion and of the Jewish way of life today, with emphasis on the rebuilding of Palestine, through which the children will be best able to fulfill their tasks at home and in synagogue, in the congregation, and in the entire Jewish community.

Without short-changing the development of all other intellectual competence, the overall educational goal should be the building of a strong and secure Jewish character. Without regard to other considerations, today's reality pushes us in this direction. The children must be prepared for possible emigration, especially to Palestine, and must be told to anticipate a difficult struggle in the future.

Consequently, great emphasis should be given to physical education; gymnastics and sports should especially be an important part of the curriculum. The anticipated change in future occupations calls for preparation in manual skills (drafting, needlework, workshop, etc.). In view of the precarious situation of Jews in Germany, the students should be offered at least one course in a modern Western language and especially instruction in modern Hebrew. (The courses must be offered in private and voluntary groups, without connection to the official curriculum.)

Religion and Hebrew

Classes in religion and Hebrew should be increased from 4 to 6 hours per week.

The purpose of Hebrew lessons is to prepare the children for participation in prayers at home, as well as in synagogue. In addition the children will be taught the skills to study important religious and secular works and be introduced to modern spoken Hebrew.

Instruction must be based on the principles of modern techniques of linguistic teaching. Grammar should be taught with emphasis on verbs and nouns to achieve an understanding of word forms. To enhance knowledge at all stages of instruction, oral and written exercises should be conducted.

The focal point of Hebrew lessons is the study of the Bible. The study of postbiblical and modern Hebrew literature should be supplemented with works of a religious slant.

History of the Bible and the Jews

Instruction in the history of the Bible and the history of the Jews constitutes an indivisible whole!

Teaching of biblical history in the lower and middle grades follows a conventional form. The presentation of religious content in the upper grades requires a second review of this history (actual reading of the Bible!) with emphasis on the law in some portions of the Torah, and the study of the

Psalms and the Prophets. It is preferable to read the appropriate passages in the original text.

In the upper grades, instruction in Jewish history is a natural continuation of Bible stories. A detailed study of the history of German Jewry is advised. Discussions of recent events are to be encouraged. The Jewish calendar with its major festivals and its minor celebrations, its religious laws, rites, and traditions, should be the subject of systematic study.

To avoid an excessive time span between general and Jewish history in one grade, synchronizing both history lessons is recommended, although they are taught in separate courses. It would be ideal if general and Jewish history, as well as Bible and Hebrew, could be taught by the same teacher.

German

Jewish schools must follow the curriculum adopted by German elementary schools.

In addition to German prose and poetry, material with a Jewish theme should be taught, either written by German-speaking authors or translated from works of the biblical or postbiblical period. Other works with significant content and form can be taught from additional material complementing the official texts and other books introduced into the course.

Local History

Knowledge of local history is the basis for acquainting the children with the world at large. The local history should include all that is relevant to Jewish life in the immediate vicinity or in more remote districts. Thus children should be prepared with an informed knowledge of Judaism.

The life of the Jewish family and society should be the topic of free discussions and should be made vivid by the customary presentations accompanying local history lessons. Celebrations of Jewish holidays should create a joyful high point in the life of the children. Local sites of interest, whether rooted in the past or connected to today's community, should be visited as part of the lessons. Starting from 4th grade, special attention should be paid to the history of the local community and the study of prominent Jewish fellow-citizens.

Geography
All grades should learn the geography of Palestine. During the study of other lands, time should be allotted to learn about the political, cultural, and economic status of the Jewish population.

Music
Music can be taught with a connection to general Jewish studies.

Attention should be given to liturgy and Hebrew songs, with the aim of enriching prayers sung in the home.

Drawing
Drawing lessons in all grades should take as their subjects the Jewish context of the children's life.

Jewish life in the home and in the community, ritual objects, biblical and other Jewish themes are ideal for graphic depictions.

The difficulties were considerable because the Jews of Bamberg had not had to deal with the specific problem of a Jewish school system since the beginning of the nineteenth century. Jewish children attended "German" schools, and if one trusts the reports of those who were pupils in this period, the only difference was that some children attended Catholic religious classes, others the Jewish ones. A Jewish curriculum (at least in Bamberg) did not exist at this time. Hence the effort of the Reichsvertretung der deutschen Juden to give the new breed of educators a helping hand. Of course in a city like Berlin, the situation was different, as can be deduced from the autobiography of Heinemann Stern. That *Judesein* ["to be a Jew"] now was different from being a Jew then was a lesson which obviously still had to be learned.

The Jewish Elementary School of Bamberg, with 38 pupils on the opening day in November 1936, was a one-room school with all the usual advantages and disadvantages. A weekly time schedule for the first year of the school's existence has survived and is reproduced in Appendix 2.

The classes conducted in the hastily set up, ill-equipped room at the synagogue at Herzog-Max St. must have been a considerable strain on students as well as teachers. The use of only one room for the school was a problem in itself, since all the pupils, regardless of age, had transferred from larger schools, where they had attended separate classes appropriate to their age group. They were not accustomed to a one-room teaching environment. Unfortunately, sources of information for this period are meager. We do not know what form life—and education—took on in the emergency school. It was by no means easy. Lost instructional time and classroom noise must have been unavoidable.

The names of the thirty-eight children who attended the Special Jewish School established at the synagogue are listed in Table 1.

TABLE 1. Students attending the Jewish elementary school

Name	Grade	Residence
Ansbacher, Jakob	8	Herzog-Max St. 13
Dingfelder, Siegfried	7	Schützen St. 27
Fleischmann, Heinz	7	Luitpold St. 48
Aigner, Ernestine	5	Pleinserhof 20
Lipp, Ilse	5	Sophien St. 9
Nussbaum, Sidonie	5	Luitpold St. 16

Sacki, Frieda	5	Hindenburgplatz 14
Schapiro, Ruth	5	Otto St. 21
Walter, Elisabeth	5	Schützen St. 23
Zeilberger, Ernst	5	Hindenburgplatz 14
Adler, Alfred	4	Kessler St. 22
Bähr, Ingeborg	4	Fleisch St. 4
Frank, Lore	4	Obere König St. 31
Kahn, Hans	4	Hain St. 15
Katz, Werner	4	Hauptwach St. 5
Löbl, Günther	4	Hain St. 16
Löbl, Johanna	4	Hain St. 17
Pauson, Eva	4	Otto St. 7
Stein, Inge	4	Schützen St. 3
Dessauer, Trude	3	Schillerplatz 18
Fleischmann, Margot	3	Kunigundendamm 23
Freudenthal, Alfred	3	Kessler St. 24
Fleischmann, Paul	3	Kunigundendamm 23
Heymann, Liselotte	3	Friedrich St. 9
Katten, Hans	3	Schillerplatz 14
Nussbaum, Manfred	3	Luitpold St. 26
Rau, Alfred	3	Hoffmann St. 2
Saalheimer, Ruth	3	Sophien St. 11
Walter, Helga	3	Luitpold St. 26
Gunzenhäuser, Ruth	2	Gangolfplatz 4
Goldschmidt, Suse	2	Luitpold St. 8
Kalischak, Edith	2	Friedrich St. 7
Katz, Ernst	2	Hauptwach St. 5
Böhm, Suse	1	Luitpold St. 47
Fleischmann, Elsbeth	1	Kunigundendamm 23
Freudenthal, Lola	1	Kessler St. 24
Löbl, Lilly	1	Hain St. 17
Nagler, Ferdinand	1	Kleber St. 11

Anyone who attended a school in temporary quarters in the postwar years can well imagine the sanitary facilities and other conditions. The city of Bamberg, officially in charge of the school, was responsible for the procurement of all material. For the most part, this was done by providing old and worn-out furnishings, as can be seen in a board of education memorandum dated April 28, 1936.

> We are faced with the procurement of used desks, blackboards, etc., for one schoolroom, items that can be found in the storerooms of many schools. . . . Perhaps there is a room available in one of the many municipal buildings, suitable for a classroom. Of course such a location must pass inspection, to comply with the sanitary rules governing school buildings. The segregated Jewish school is still part of the public school system, at least until the announcement of new national regulations.

A list of the modest furnishings finally allocated, reads as follows:

> 10 desks (5 with 3 seats and 5 with 4 seats)
> 1 cabinet
> 1 teacher's desk with hinged cover and wooden platform
> 1 chair
> 1 geophysical map of Germany
> 1 map of Southern Germany
> 1 map of Palestine
> 1 map of Upper Franconia
> several visual-aid pictures on canvas (3m x 5m)
> 3 teaching manuals for elementary schools (grades 3–4, 5–6, and 7–8)
> 3 arithmetic books
> school forms (student files, student lists, teaching records, scheduling plans)
> 1 ruler
> 1 inkwell
> 1 lamp

1 blackboard with easel
1 large wall blackboard
1 sandbox
1 wastebasket

The congregational chronicle took note of the establishment of the Special Jewish School:

> *Nov. 6.* Special classes for Jewish children in the public elementary school system opened. Thirty-eight children in 7 grades are enrolled. Mr. Justin Frankel, Erlangen, was appointed to the position as teacher. The government of Upper Franconia hired Mr. Frankel under a contract without pension rights and dismissal on 4 months notice. The city pays the salary. The school premises are the former conference room in the synagogue. Fixtures are the property of the city.

In the final analysis, education in the two years from November 1936 to November 1938 was merely a makeshift operation. The added threat of "national regulations" was a dark cloud over the entire enterprise. It was easy to imagine what such regulations would entail.

Difficulties with the meager teaching staff defeated any attempt at successful education. The worst part was the arrest of Justin Frankel in April 1937, and his incarceration until November of that year. After his release he decided not to return to his position. Starting April 29, a Jewish teacher-in-training, Ludwig Fleischmann, assumed the position of full-time teacher. Due to his lack of experience, the chances of his permanent appointment were very slim. Later on Possenheimer and Neumann applied, but their permanent employment ran into difficulties. On November 1, 1937, the chairman of the education committee, Dr. Martin Morgenroth, wrote to the Bamberg Board of Education: "The parents of the student body of the Special Jewish School question the status of the school constantly and want to be assured of a speedy decision on the final disposition of this institution."

Furthermore, there was a nagging problem concerning the position of a trained teacher of needlework courses. At first a trained needlework teacher in Bamberg was approached, but she refused the position, citing serious reasons. Another gentile teacher, who accepted the position, was forced to resign because Aryan teachers were not allowed to teach Jews. Starting in April, an uncertified Jewish teacher of needlework, Elisabeth Awrach, took over the courses.

With the destruction of the synagogue on November 9–10, 1938, the classroom lay in ruins. For a long time there was no schooling for Jewish children in Bamberg. The national law, long anticipated with apprehension, took effect on November 15, 1938. The National Ministry of Education decreed the complete expulsion of Jewish pupils from the entire school system of the German Reich. From now on Jewish students were only allowed to attend Jewish schools. This released the Bamberg municipality from all responsibility for a special Jewish school. The defeated Jewish community of Bamberg was now forced to provide a private school with material and personnel, while still waiting for an official permit. To put it into a clearer and truer light: on January 6, 1939, the congregation applied for a license to open a private school but never received a response from the school authorities. On April 23, the Union of Jewish Congregations of Bavaria appealed directly to the Ministry of Culture, describing the situation in Bamberg.

> We take the liberty of referring to a visit to your offices at the beginning of April. At that time we petitioned for a permit to open a private Jewish elementary school in Bamberg. This action was necessitated by the dire need for schooling of the Jewish youth of Bamberg. According to reports from the congregation of Bamberg, the complete lack of education

becomes increasingly evident. Said congregation begs to inform you of the parents' request, at the least, to permit religious instruction for their children. A discussion with the school chancellor of Bamberg concerning this matter led to no results, according to the congregation's report. The chancellor explained that he does not know whether religious instruction is a required subject in a Jewish private school as it is in state-chartered schools, or if religious instruction in Jewish schools is exempt from state regulations. We again appeal to the highest authorities to permit a full teaching schedule at a Jewish private school in Bamberg. In case of any obstacles, we beg permission, at least, for religious instruction.

On May 16, 1939 a private school was approved:

The Jewish congregation of Bamberg is hereby given permission to open and operate a private elementary school on the premises of the Jewish Old-Age Home, Zinkenwörth 17. This permit is revocable and governed by the following statutes:

(a) The establishment shall operate under the name "Private Elementary School of the Jewish Congregation of Bamberg."

(b) The entire school supply, professional and personal, is the responsibility of the congregation. Supervision and instruction is in the hands of the former Jewish assistant teacher Paul Possenheimer, Bamberg. This position can be revoked at any time.

The documents tell us very little about the school at the White Dove Inn. It is known that Samuel Palm taught English, and Master Tailor Irma Walter, needlework.

The deportations, starting at the end of November 1941, put an end to all school activities in Bamberg. We do not know to what extent classes were able to function in the period between the outbreak of the war and the beginning of the deportations. Regulations issued by the Ministry of Science and Education and the Headquarters for National Security (dated June 20, 1942 and July 7, 1942), albeit never officially published, completely terminated the Jewish school system in the German Reich.

> The Reichsvereinigung of Jews in Germany is advised that as of June 30, 1942 all Jewish schools must be closed. The membership must be notified that beginning July 1, 1942 all schooling of Jewish children is prohibited. This order is given in view of the recent resettlement of Jews.

NOTE

The section of this chapter covering the Special Jewish Schools is mainly based on documents from the state offices of the Bamberg board of education. The files contained records on the registration of school-age Jewish children and the establishment of a segregated school in the room at the synagogue building; · also a number of school records, mostly of students born in 1924 and 1925. The file also contained a copy of the guidelines for the creation of a curriculum for the Jewish elementary schools. Teachers who worked for decades in one-room schoolhouses are of the opinion that this type of schooling has some advantages, but only if teacher and student "grow up" in the system. The segregated school in Bamberg did not fit this description. The sandbox mentioned in the inventory was an indispensable tool of primary education in the 1920s and 1930s. It was used for recreating terrain as an aid in teaching geography and local history, similar to the exercises at a war college.

Heinemann Stern, in his *Why Do They Really Hate Us?* (Düsseldorf, 1970), describes the difficulties of establishing a Jewish school system in the Third Reich. Stern was a leader in the Centralverein of German Citizens of the Jewish Faith, and until his emigration in 1941, the headmaster of a Jewish middle school for boys in Berlin.

The regulations issued by the Minister of Science and Education (E II e Nr 1598) are documented by Joseph Walk in *Separate Justice for Jews in the Nazi State* (Heidelberg/Karlsruhe, 1981).

2

The Pogrom of November 1938

THE NAME REICHSKRISTALLNACHT, of unknown origin but most likely coined in Berlin, was given to the events now to be described. Based on all the accumulated evidence, it was a spontaneous decision of the Reichsminister for Information and Propaganda, with the consent of Hitler, that led to this operation against Jews throughout the Reich during the night of November 9–10, 1938. The official pretext was an attempt on the life of an attaché at the German embassy in Paris by a young Polish Jew. This incident was proclaimed an attack by world Jewry against the German nation.

Whatever happened was done under the pretense of a spontaneous reaction of the populace, an explosion of the people's rage, yet in reality, despite the short time for preparations, the operation was well planned. The timing was perfect, because on this evening veterans throughout the nation were commemorating the anniversary of Hitler's attempted putsch in Munich in 1923. The necessary manpower was already assembled and, through inflammatory speeches and drunkenness, easily whipped into action.

We know what happened in Bamberg thanks to a trial in 1946, held at the District Court, that diligently prosecuted the perpetrators. Because of extensive testimony by participants, as well as by "innocent" bystanders, the course of events was easily traced.

On the evening of November 9, mandatory meetings of party members took place at the Zentralsaal and the Luitpold Hall. During the day reports of the death of the victim of the Paris assassination attempt became common knowledge in the city, and in his speeches at both meetings District Leader and Lord Mayor Lorenz Zahneisen called on the Jews of Bamberg to disappear.

While these meetings were still in progress, members of the Hitler Youth began to paint graffiti such as slogans like JEWS SCRAM, JEW PIG, and DEATH TO THE JEWS on Jewish buildings, in particular the synagogue. The police wanted to intervene but were told that the district leader had given his express permission.

After the meetings party members congregated in a number of taverns for more drinks; the leaders met in an exclusive restaurant, well known to this day. At this location (around midnight) the district leader received a telephone call from party headquarters in Bayreuth with the "order to attack." He ordered all unit leaders present (SA [storm troopers], SS [security detachments], and NSKK [Nazi motor corps]) into an adjoining room and announced the order from above: to destroy all synagogues in the district. He answered the objections of some of those present by stating that everything was absolutely legitimate. The police would not interfere; their phone lines would be closed to incoming calls. He also ordered the complete destruction of the community center and restaurant at the White Dove Inn.

According to investigations, the leaders, with little help from the rank and file, initiated the activities at the synagogue. But an operation of such magnitude did not remain a secret. SA and SS troops, still celebrating in a number of taverns downtown, were alerted by telephone and messenger. A considerable mob of men in uniform converged on Herzog-Max Street, either as spectators or as active participants.

From a nearby garage crowbars and hammers were obtained and then used to break down the synagogue's doors. Even before this a few men gained entrance through a broken window on the south side of the building and poured gasoline into the main sanctuary of the synagogue in preparation for arson. Smashed fixtures and curtains were used as kindling. Additional fires were started in the foyer and cloakroom and finally in the balcony.

The fire brigade (summoned by neighbors) arrived on the scene at 1:20 a.m. The district leader confronted the fire chief, asked him what he thought he was doing, and told him that there was nothing to be extinguished; the most he could do was to protect neighboring buildings. A district attorney on the scene advised the fire chief not to meddle in matters of no concern to him. Nevertheless, the first fire company to arrive tried to enter the synagogue with a high-pressure hose, but encountered SS and NSKK men, obviously intoxicated, and was forcefully ejected. An attempt to put out the fire on the north side of the synagogue was personally stopped by the district leader.

At the trial in 1946 a member of the fire brigade testified that the effort of the firefighters deteriorated into a farce, for show only. The many sources of fire in the interior of the building combined into a conflagration and around 3:00 a.m. the flames broke through the roof. The next morning uniformed Nazis were still attempting to set fire to parts of the building not yet incinerated; but they failed.

Besides arson and destruction of buildings, shops, and residences, other things happened that night. There was violence against persons. Around 2:00 a.m. Councillor Willy Lessing of Sophien Street 6, trustee of the Jewish congregation, received a telephone call informing him of the incidents at the synagogue.

He tried to get there at once. He was stopped at the barriers erected on Urban Street, near a tavern called Inn of the Green Wreath. Some bystanders recognized him and alerted a Nazi officer to his presence. The latter hit Willy Lessing in the chest and, using abusive language, chased him to the corner of Herzog-Max and Amalien Streets. Four or five Nazis in uniform struck him in the face with their fists and kicked him with their boots. He was forced to repeat, "I am a dirty Jew, a Jew pig, a stinking Jew," and was again kicked.

Severely injured, Lessing hastily returned home. At this point his condition·was already cause for concern. But at 2:30 a.m. more men, some in uniform, others in civilian clothes, entered his home, calling him a "dirty Jew" and "Jew pig," and dragged him from the house while constantly beating him. On the way out he was cruelly mistreated and finally left lying in front of Sophien Street 4. While all this was going on, others tried to start a fire in the lobby of the building by igniting a basket full of wood shavings. The ensuing flames were soon extinguished. Willy Lessing died on January 17, 1939; he never recovered from the beatings.

Back at the synagogue the mob of spectators increased by leaps and bounds. Small bands formed, consisting both of men in uniform and men in civilian clothes. Stirred up and incited by the speeches during the evening and the events of the night, they entered Jewish houses and apartments and dragged the residents into the street, abusing them as they did so. A case in point—one of many—is the house at Hain Street 14. Around 3:00 a.m. four men gained entry by breaking a window and chased the occupants, Otto Kahn and his wife, down the back stairs. Mrs. Kahn, in an attempt to protect her husband, tried to grab the SA dagger that one of the intruders waved in their faces and cut her hand. (The next day the proud owner of the dagger showed it to his co-workers in the shop where he was employed with the boast: "This is Jew blood on the blade.") Otto Kahn was beaten in front of his house and left unconscious.

Another band ran wild at the White Dove at Zinkenwörth, destroyed all the furniture, and had to be prevented from torching the building.

The smell caused by the burning synagogue hung over Herzog-Max Street early in the morning of November 10. Idle curiosity-seekers had to be restrained by police barriers. Those Bambergers who did not know that the synagogue was burning learned of it on the way to work or school. Everybody wanted to have at least a quick look. Burning ruins were—at least in those days—a rare sight.

The government offices were a beehive of activity, especially the police department. The "spontaneous riot" and its aftermath needed a semblance of legality. Orders came down from Berlin to "take all Jews over the age of 18 into protective custody." And that is exactly what happened in the city as well as in the smaller communities in the district. Bamberg's prison on Sand Street was filled to capacity. According to a list compiled by the political police (dated November 11), 81 men from Bamberg alone were booked; to this were added 26 men from the surrounding district. All were held for transfer to the concentration camp at Dachau.

Official documents made no mention of the "searches" of residences and their consequences, with the exception of an occasional veiled reference. Of course descriptions by victims give a very clear picture of this side of the "protest riots." A constable from Lichtenfels coined a puzzling name for the riots: *Entgärungsaktion*—"riots caused by fermentation."

To arrive at a better picture let us look at some official documents, such as this one from the local police:

Police Department of the City of Bamberg
Department P.

No. 3047Bamberg, November 11, 1938
Enclosure: 1 list

I. After disclosure of the death of the German diplomat
vom Rath, murdered by a cowardly Jewish assassin, anti-Jewish demonstrations developed on the evening of Nov. 9, 1938
and the night of Nov. 9–10, 1938 in the city of Bamberg.

The rage of the agitated populace led to the complete
destruction of the Jewish restaurant and youth hostel at the
White Dove Inn.

Around 1:00 a.m. a fire started in the synagogue of Bamberg and fed by wooden furnishings soon engulfed the entire
interior. The building was completely destroyed by fire. During the night several Jews provoked the enraged masses by
appearing on the streets. This led to the temporary detention
of all Jewish males in Bamberg by the police. There were no
instances of looting.

During the morning hours of Nov. 10, 1938 additional
Jewish males were taken into custody and held at the local
district prison. As per order from the Secret State Police,
Nuremberg, this group was transferred into the hands of the
camp administration of Dachau. On the night of Nov. 10–
11, 1938, at 2:57 a.m., 81 men departed for Dachau by
express train, as per orders received.

Regarding the fire at the synagogue, a complaint was
lodged by the Bureau of the State Police with the district
attorney against unknown arsonists.

A list of Jewish deportees is enclosed.

Remarkable reports arrived from constabulary posts throughout the district—remarkable because of their obscure, yet
revealing, language. These documents cry out to be read
between the lines. The constabulary post in Schesslitz submit-

ted the following weekly report on November 11, 1938, concerning the riots in Demmelsdorf and Zeckendorf (supposedly with the participation of men from Bamberg):

> After it became known that the German diplomat vom Raht [*sic*], shot at by a Jewish scoundrel, had succumbed to his injuries, synagogues were burned in revenge during the night of Nov. 10, 1938 in Demmelsdorf and Zeckendorf, where Jews still reside. The general public showed their indignation in various degrees. . . . No attacks against Jewish buildings and businesses occurred. There are no known claims of abuse of Jews. Reports of above-mentioned events reached the station about 6:00 a.m. the next morning.

What kind of police are these? Two synagogues in their jurisdiction are destroyed, but it is only many hours after the incidents occur that these facts are brought to their attention. The statement that there were no known reports of mistreatment of Jews may well be interpreted to mean that the otherwise extremely alert Schesslitz constabulary was not notified of any abuses. A letter from the district commissioner in Bamberg is a case in point:

December 7, 1938

To the Administration of the Bamberg General Hospital:
Re: Bill for the Jew Ludwig Heimann, Demmelsdorf
Enclosure: 1 invoice

> Enclosed you will find the bill dated Dec. 5, 1938, returned to you with a request to bill Ludwig Heimann directly for all medical expenses incurred. The state will not reimburse individual Jews for expenses incurred due to retaliatory measures against all Jewry. . . .

Some towns in the district hastened events on their own initiative, as seen in Aschbach, where on November 7, between 12:30 and 1:00 a.m., at the house of Jakob Seeman (a disabled war veteran on pension) the shutters of two ground-floor windows of his bedroom were forced open and the window panes broken. Through these shattered windows the following items were thrown: 7 logs of firewood, 1 pine branch, 2 wooden sticks, and 1 stone the size of a child's head. At the same time, two windows of the ground-floor kitchen at the house of the Jewish merchant Meier Bayer in Aschbach were broken. The following perpetrators were apprehended: F.B., 20, single, laborer . . . L.N., 17, single, laborer . . . B.K., 27, single, ditch digger. . . . Questioned about motives, they replied that anger about the murder by a Jew of our ambassador in Paris had triggered the reaction to smash windows of Jews in Aschbach.

So much for the report of "premature" revenge by the Burgwindheim constabulary. These incidents are too remote in time for their backgbround to be clarified. There may have been a private vendetta; but quite evidently the alleged murder of our ambassador was used as a pretext for many sins. Vom Rath was not an ambassador and was still alive on November 7. The report from the Burgwindheim constabulary is dated November 24.

Arrests in Bamberg, starting during the night, continued into the morning of November 10. Photos show Jews being led through the streets by police and SA men, on the way to Sand Street, but do not show any participation by the general public. There are no curious onlookers in the pictures. The impression remains that this was just a common daily occurrence.

There are reports of cases where arrested Jews tried to calm their alarmed gentile neighbors. They used the prevailing argument, widespread in the Germany of those days: "We served in the army, we fought for Germany; all this is a misunderstanding, nothing can happen to us, *not to us.*" This argument did not stand up. War veterans and "civilians" alike wound up in the prison on Sand Street. There it became clear—slowly but surely—that the arrests and all the other abuses suffered during the night were not misunderstandings. On the afternoon of November 11 the transport left for Dachau.

Found among the surviving documents in the Bamberg office of the state police is a "List of Jews Arrested during the Protest Riots in Bamberg on Nov. 11, 1938 and Transferred to the Dachau Concentration Camp":

1. Adler, Moritz, clerk, born Oct. 1, 1897, Gebweiler, Jew,[1] married to Elvira, née Fostel, son of Nathan and Sonny, née Schloss. Bamberg, Kessler St. 18.
2. Aigner, Josef, engraver, born Aug. 30, 1884, Munich, Jew, married to Berta, née Singer, son of Johann and Walburga, née Merz. Bamberg, Pleinserhof 20.
3. Ansbacher, Leo, custodian, born Mar. 20, 1887, Zeckendorf near Bamberg, Jew, married to Rosa, née Hofmann, son of Jakob and Sofie, née Wurzmann. Bamberg, Herzog-Max St. 13.
4. Banemann, Justin, merchant, born July 20, 1880, Burgkunstadt, Jew, married to Ida, née Freitag, son of Adolf and Rosa, née Steinhäuser. Bamberg, Luitpold St. 48.
5. Batt, Arthur, manager, born Aug. 15, 1895, Rogasen/ Posen, Jew, married to Gertrud, née Bartelt, son of Wolf and Hedwig, née Kallmann. Bamberg, Geyerswörth St. 8.
6. Berg, Norbert, salesman, born Aug. 15, 1895, Warburg/ Westf., Jew, single, son of Meinhard and Selma, née Nathanson. Bamberg, Maxplatz 14.
7. Brandes, Sally, merchant, born Jan. 4, 1882, Rothenburg/Fulda, Jew, married to Berta, née Herstein, son of

---

1 In the original document, the abbreviation *R.D.* (probably *Reichsdeutsch*, i.e., German citizen) appears in each entry at this point. (Ed.)

Hirsch and Hannchen, née Herrmann. Bamberg, Herzog-Max St. 16.

8. Bütow, Selmar, bookkeeper, born Nov. 13, 1884, Hellsberg, East Prussia, Jew, married to Frieda, née Jakobsohn, son of Gabriel and Hulda, née Moses. Bamberg, Friedrich St. 7

9. Dingfelder, Ignatz, cattle dealer, born Mar. 4, 1891, Uhlfeld, Jew, married to Marta, née Schwab, son of Seligmann and Emma, née Hellmann. Bamberg, Luisen St. 3.

10. Dingfelder, Ludwig, cattle dealer, born Apr. 10, 1888, Uhlfeld, Jew, single, son of Seligmann and Emma, née Hellmann. Bamberg, Luisen Str. 3.

11. Ehrlich, Max, merchant, born June 16, 1880, Oberaltersheim, Jew, married to Lina, née Stein, son of Samuel and Jette, née Ullmann. Bamberg, Herzog-Max Str. 3.

12. Fein, Max, merchant, born June 16, 1880, Oberaltersheim, Jew, married to Recha, née Reuss, son of Simon and Sara, née Kaufmann. Bamberg, Kunigundendamm 3.

13. Fleischmann, Gustav, horse dealer, born July 7, 1891, Prichsenstadt near Gerolshofen, Jew, married to Margareta, née Cahn, son of Hermann and Johanna, née Klein. Bamberg, Kunigundendamm 20.

14. Fleischmann, Ludwig, merchant, born Feb. 24, 1886, Hofheim, Jew, married to Ida, née Reuss, son of Josef and Henriette, née Stern. Bamberg, Kunigundendamm 23.

15. Fleischmann, Oskar, born Mar. 9, 1882, Forchheim, Jew, married to Paula, née Mayer, son of Isidor and Auguste, née Schwarzmann. Bamberg, Otto St. 15.

16. Fleissig, August, merchant, born Oct. 5, 1897, Bamberg, Jew, married to Elsa, née Löwenthal, son of Hermann and Frederika, née Goldmann. Bamberg, Obere König St. 8

17. Florsheim, Herbert, apprentice baker, born Apr. 11,

1920, Jew, single, son of Nathan and Selma, née Stiefel. Bamberg, Adolf Hitler St. 35.

18. Forchheimer, Adolf, merchant, born Dec. 1, 1884, Thüngen, Jew, married to Rosa, née Michels, son of Öskar and Caroline, née Heinemann. Bamberg, Au St. 21.

19. Forchheimer, Isidor, merchant, born Apr. 22, 1887, Thüngen, Jew, married to Johanna, née Michels, son of Oskar and Caroline, née Heinemann. Bamberg, Kessler St. 18.

20. Frank, Gustav, merchant, born July 1, 1890, Memmelsdorf, Lower Franconia, Jew, married to Frieda, née Schweizer, son of Simon and Rita, née Freundlich. Bamberg, Hauptwach St. 14.

21. Frank, Heinz, clerk, born Mar. 24, 1919, Bamberg, Jew, single, son of Siegfried and Tina, née Früh. Bamberg, Franz-Ludwig St. 26.

22. Frank, Max, merchant, born Jan. 9, 1887, Saalfeld, Jew, married to Rita, née Friedmann, son of Moritz and Sofie, née Rosenberger. Bamberg, Luitpold St. 4.

23. Frank, Moritz, cattle dealer, Sept. 21, 1895, Wonfurt, Jew, single, son of Josef and Hannchen, née Neuburger. Bamberg, Untere König St. 2.

24. Freudenthal, Viktor, butcher, born Nov. 10, 1895, Altenkunstadt, Jew, married to Elsa, née Guth, son of Lehmann and Rosa, née Levor. Bamberg, Kessler St. 24.

25. Gerst, Hans, merchant, born Dec. 31, 1886, Bamberg, Jew, married to Irma, née Silbermann, son of Moritz and Dora, née Gütermann. Bamberg, Sofien St. 10.

26. Goldmann, Manfred, hops dealer, born Apr. 26, 1885, Bamberg, Jew, married to Hedwig, née Wertheimer, son of Salomon and Hannchen, née Strauss. Bamberg, Heinrichsdamm 7.

27. Grausmann, Fritz, merchant, born Dec. 21, 1892, Bamberg, Jew, married to Antonie, née Riesenfelder, son of Moritz and Eva, née Wachtel. Bamberg, Sofien St. 5.

28. Grünebaum, Moritz, merchant, born Jun. 28, 1899, Niederwern near Schweinfurt, Jew, married to Johanna, née Mayer, son of Mayers and Nanny, née May. Bamberg, Schützen St. 16.

29. Gunzenhäuser, Emil, merchant, born Dec. 16, 1883, Memmelsdorf, Lower Franconia, Jew, married to Johanna, née Früh, son of Moritz and Tina, née Hessdorfer. Bamberg, Luitpold St. 41.

30. Herrmann, Gustav, salesman, born Sept. 22, 1887, Schesslitz, Jew, single, son of Ludwig and Ernestine, née Fleischer. Bamberg, Heiliggrab 4.

31. Herrmann, Sigmund, cattle dealer, born July 14, 1894, Schesslitz, Jew, single, son of Ludwig and Ernestine, née Fleischer. Bamberg, Heiliggrab 4.

32. Hess, Artur, merchant, born May 5, 1911, Bamberg, Jew, single, son of Wilhelm and Else, née Leopold. Bamberg, Au St. 14.

33. Hess, Friedrich, merchant, born Aug. 7, 1902, Bamberg, Jew, married to Emilie, née Hofer, son of Leopold and Selma, née Schwarzhaupt. Bamberg, Hain St. 29.

34. Hess, Wilhelm, merchant, born July 12, 1881, Bischberg near Bamberg, Jew, married to Else, née Leopold, son of Lippmann and Babette, née Wolfenstein. Bamberg, Au St. 14.

35. Hessberg, Alfred, merchant, born Jan. 2, 1884, Bamberg, Jew, single, son of Heinrich and Henriette, née Frank. Bamberg, Friedrich St. 9.

36. Jakobsohn, Erich, manager, born Feb. 7, 1902, Pillau, Jew, married to Margareta née Simon, son of Georg and Frieda, née Ruginski. Bamberg, Hain St. 17.

37. Isner, Simon, clerk, born July 6, 1904, Saugen/Memmel, Jew, single, son of Nison and Ida, née Rosenberg. Bamberg, Schützen St. 11.

38. Isner, Emil, merchant, born July 30, 1880, Burghasslach near Scheinfeld, Jew, married to Hedwig, née Bayreuther, son of Benno and Maria, née Breuer. Bam-

berg, Luitpold St. 16.

39. Kahn, Otto, merchant, born Nov. 11, 1884, Bamberg, Jew, married to Rosa, née Schubart, son of Louis and Fanny, née Grünfelder. Bamberg, Main St. 14.

40. Kahn, Sally, manufacturer, born May 27, 1885, Gleicherwiesen near Röhmhild, Jew, son of the merchant Anselm and Berta, née Cramer, married to Dora, née Fleissig. Bamberg, Hain St. 15.

41. Kalischak, Richard, merchant, born May 27, 1885, Plauen, Jew, married to Else, née Mossbacher, son of Sally and Cecilie, née Mannheimer. Bamberg, Friedrich St. 7

42. Katten, Max, Rabbi, born Oct. 5, 1892, Bonn/Pappelsdorf, Jew, married to Wilma, née Guttmann, son of Salomon and Nanny, née Moses. Bamberg, Schillerplatz 14.

43. Kaumheimer, Fritz, journeyman gardener, born Sept. 20, 1919, Berlin, Jew, single, son of Heinrich and Johanna, née Kohler. Bamberg, Zinkenwörth 17.

44. Kohn, Ignaz, merchant, born Apr. 9, 1886, Burgkunstadt, Jew, married to Rosa, née Dorn, on of Karl and Gertrud, née Dingfelder. Bamberg, Luitpold St. 48.

45. Kronacher Josef, merchant, born Feb. 24, 1881, Bamberg, Jew, married to Karola, née Nasser, son of Simon and Siegelinde, née Lehmann. Bamberg, Schützen St. 30.

46. Kugelmann, Erich,, journeyman gardener, born July 29, 1910, Bremen, Jew, single, son of Gustav and Beate, née Netheim. Bamberg, Zinkenwörth 17.

47. Kuhn, Philip, butcher, born Dec. 6, 1889, Altenschönbach near Gerolzhofen, Jew, married to Helene, née Schmidt, son of Lehmann and Elise, née Stern. Bamberg, Luitpold St. 41.

48. Lang, Ludwig, merchant, born Feb. 13, 1881, Eschwege/Werra, Jew, widower, son of Siegmund and Seravine, née Katzenstein. Bamberg, Luisen St. 2.

49. Lein, Heinrich, merchant, born Jan. 11, 1884, Diespeck, Jew, married to Dekla, née Weinmann, son of Albert and Sofie, née Dingfelder. Bamberg, Promenade St. 4.

50. Lindner, Herbert, merchant, born Nov. 11, 1897, Burgkunstadt, Jew, married to Mathilde, née Kochenthlaer, son of Oskar and Gertrud, née Feuchtwanger. Bamberg, Schützen St. 5.

51. Lipp, Heinrich, merchant, born Aug. 6, 1886, Bamberg, Jew, married to Mathilde, née Reichmannsdorfer, son of Israel and Mathilde, née Maier. Bamberg, Sofien St. 9.

52. Löbl, Sally, merchant, born Nov. 4, 1890, Bamberg, Jew, married to Frieda, née Aufhäuser, son of Hugo and Lina, née Schloss. Bamberg, Luitpold St. 27.

53. Manasse, Ernst, carpenter, born Aug. 22, 1905, Halle/Saale, Jew, married to Irene, née Rosenthal, son of Louis and Hedwig, née Grabe. Bamberg, Zinkenwörth 17.

54. Mohrenwitz, Stefan manufacturer, born Mar. 26, 1883, Bamberg, Jew, married to Ida née Reichmann, son of Bernhard and Antonie, née Bing. Bamberg, Hain St. 22.

55. Naumann, Ludwig, merchant, born Dec. 15, 1906, Bischberg, Jew, single, son of Hermann & Fanny, née Hess. Bamberg, Adolf Hitler St. 18.

56. Neuburger, Ernst, manufacturer, born Mar. 31, 1881, Fürth, Jew, single, son of Josef and Josefine, née Kohn. Bamberg, Schützen St. 1.

57. Dr. Oster, Ludwig, attorney, born Aug. 2, 1882, Bamberg, Jew, single, son of Moses and Marianne, née Hartmann. Bamberg, Adolf Hitler St. 33.

58. Pauson, Stefan, merchant, born Mar. 23, 1887, Lichtenfels, Jew, married to Helene, née Herzfelder, son of Pankraz and Rosa, née Fechheimer. Bamberg, Otto St. 7,

59. Possenheim, Karl, teacher, born July 19, 1913, Burgkunstadt, Jew, single, son of Max and Bella, née Löwenstein. Bamberg, Franz-Ludwig St. 26.

60. Pretzfelder, Paul, merchant, born Oct. 2, 1906, Burgkunstadt, Jew, married to Margot, née Sternglanz, son of

Max and Lissy, née Süssenmuth. Bamberg, Friedrich St, 10.

61. Reichmannsdorfer, Isidor, merchant, born Apr. 10, 1884, Trabelsdorf, Jew, single, son of Heinrich and Babette, née Cohn. Bamberg, Au St. 23.

62. Rindsberg, Ernst, cattle dealer, born Sept. 11, 1897, Bamberg, Jew,single, son of Moses ,and Hannchen, née Traub. Bamberg, Josef St. 14B.

63. Rossheimer, Stefan, merchant, born July 8, 1905, Bamberg, Jew, married to Erna, née Marx, son of Hugo and Rosa, née Kaufmann. Bamberg, Luitpold St, 50.

64. Saalheimer, Justus, merchant, born Aug. 24, 1887, Bamberg, Jew, married to Gretchen, née Bickart, son of Max and Sidonie, née Österlein. Bamberg, Sofien St. 11.

65. Schaffrainsky, Rudi, trainée, born Apr. 21, 1916, Berlin, Jew, son of Salomon and Rosa, née Fenster. Bamberg, Zinkenwörth 17.

66. Schapiro, Julius, teacher, born Feb. 1, 1895, Burghasslach, Jew, married to Nora, née Hahn, son of Samuel and Caroline, née Fuchtler. Bamberg, Kessler St. 18.

67. Schloss, Simon, merchant, born Aug. 31, 1880, Gunzendorf near Bamberg, Jew, married to Martha, née Dingfelder, son of Hermann and Helene, née Heumann. Bamberg, Franz Ludwig St. 24.

68. Schütz, Josef, merchant, born Aug. 31, 1880, Hirschaid, Jew, married to Gretl, née Spier, son of Wilhelm and Theresia, née Reiss. Bamberg, Luitpold St. 23.

69. Silbermann, Ernst, merchant, born Mar. 8, 1907, Bamberg, Jew, single, son of William and Lina, née Steinheimer. Bamberg, Sofien St. 10.

70. Silbermann, Leo, waiter., born Feb. 3, 1915, Oberelsbach, Jew, single, son of Heinrich and Babette, née Hahnlein. Bamberg, Zinkenwörth 17.

71. Spier, Josef, salesman, born Jan. 13, 1900, Landshut, Jew, married to Planka, née Meyer, son of Max and Henriette, née Wilmersdörfer. Bamberg, Luitpold St. 4.

72. Steiner, Kurt, merchant, born May 6, 1898, Breslau, Jew, single, son of Heinrich and Frederike, née Rosenthal. Bamberg, Dietrich Eckart St. 5.
73. Sternglanz, Albert, merchant, born Jan. 3, 1883, Stuttgart, Jew, married to Schene, née Fleissig, son of David and Sery, née Alexander. Bamberg, Sofien St. 11.
74. Stoll, Moses, baker, born Nov. 7, 1880, Massbach near Schweinfurt, Jew, married to Berta, née Grünebaum, son of Meier and Fanny, née Meier. Bamberg, Adolf Hitler St. 35.
75. Strauss, Sally, merchant, born Aug. 16, 1903, Mittelsinn near Gemünden, Jew, single, son of Juda and Emma, née Rothschild. Bamberg, Friedrich St. 6.
76. Traub, Isidor, merchant, born Oct. 10, 1883, Trunstadt near Bamberg, Jew, single, son of Abraham and Klara, née Josef. Bamberg, Josef St. 14b
77. Triest, Willy, merchant, born Jan. 20, 1879, Bamberg, Jew, single, son of Ferdinand and Sara, née Haas. Bamberg, Luitpold St. 25.
78. Walter, Isidor, merchant, born Oct. 8, 1880, Sugenheim near Scheinfeld, Jew, married to Rosa, née Früh, son of Abraham and Babette, née Selling. Bamberg, Schützen St. 23.
79. Wassermann, Kurt, electrical enginéer, born May 12, 1907, Bamberg, Jew, single, son of Karl and Martha, née Nathanson. Bamberg, Dietrich Eckart St. 7.
80. Wetzlar, Max, jeweler, born Nov. 22, 1879, Bamberg, Jew, married to Frieda, née Thiele, son of Salomon and Pauline, née Klein. Bamberg, Härtlein St. 7.
81. Wiesenfelder, Max, manufacturer, born Feb. 20, 1909, Bamberg, Jew, married to Tilli, née Rehbock, son of Josef and Rosa, née Gunzenhäuser. Bamberg, Friedrich St. 6.

The roundups stopped and a final report (dated November 26) explains the entire affair as seen through the eyes of the political police in Bamberg. Bezold, who signed the document, was most likely its author.

Office of the State Police
Secret
Department P.

No. 3199   Bamberg, Nov. 26, 1938

Re: Summary and final report on the protest riots against Jews in the precincts of the city of Bamberg, Nov. 9–10, 1938.

Enclosure: Inventory

1. On Nov. 7, 1938, as the news of an attempt on the life of attaché Dr. vom Rath at the German embassy in Paris spread through Bamberg, it caused enormous agitation and anger. All over town groups of citizens congregated and discussed the events. At the disclosure of the death of Mr. vom Rath (on the evening of Nov. 9, 1938), open threats against Jews were heard everywhere.

Around 1:00 a.m. (Nov. 10, 1938), a fire broke out in the Bamberg synagogue and, fed by wooden furnishings, soon engulfed the entire interior. The building was completely gutted on the inside and, save for the outer walls, was a total ruin. The extension on the left side of the relatively large building (including the custodian's residence) escaped the conflagration, but his apartment had to be demolished.

Furthermore the interior of the Jewish White Dove Inn, at Zinkenwörth 17, was smashed, causing the destruction of the offices of the Jewish community and the home of Hechalutz [the Jewish Pioneer organization].

Department P of the state police received cash and objects of value found in the synagogue and the White Dove:

(a) White Dove:
1 box containing 75.40 reichmarks
1 closed collection box for the Jewish Winter Relief; contents unknown
1 cigar box containing 746.70 reichmarks
1 uncashed check in the amount of 1,285.00 reichmarks
postage stamps totaling 15.49 reichmarks
1 envelope containing 180 reichmarks
(b) Synagogue:
1 envelope containing 185 reichmarks

The above cash and valuables are in safekeeping with the Bamberg police inspector.

The White Dove Inn was closed and the building is under the care of the custodian, Albert Schlossheimer, residing at the same location.

The offices containing the undamaged safe were sealed by the police.

Property damage at the White Dove is estimated at between 500 and 600 reichmarks.

The synagogue is covered by fire insurance in the estimated amount of 700,000 reichmarks.

One ton of rare books, prayer books, accounting files, and correspondence found at the synagogue and the White Dove was secured and is in safekeeping with department P.

The district office and the city administration made no definite decision on the ultimate fate of the synagogue. However, there is imminent danger of collapse of the synagogue building due to bending and melting of supporting iron beams exposed to very high temperatures.

The home for Hechalutz in the White Dove was disbanded; the restaurant was also closed. No decisions were reached concerning the final use of this property.

At the time of the protest riots, Bamberg still had about 80 Jewish stores, offices, and business concerns, many of them in the process of transfer into Aryan hands. The only damage to a store occurred at H & C Tietz, where a plate-glass window was broken. Other establishments were only defaced by graffiti. Out of fear, as recently as today, Jewish establishments kept their shops closed.

Of the approximately 280 Jewish residences in Bamberg, none showed property damage caused by the riots. Foreign citizens suffered no harm.

Also, no Aryans were affected by the protest riots.

As of now, no claims of theft have been submitted by Jews.

The only incident of serious abuse during the riots involved the Jew Wilhelm Lessing of Bamberg, residing at Sofien St. 8, Bamberg. Lessing attempted to reach the synagogue during the fire and was beaten by people at the scene.

During the night of November 9–10, 1938 the Jewess Gretchen Bing, née Hesslein, born Dec. 20, 1872, in Bamberg, and residing at Luitpold St. 40, committed suicide by ingesting veronal.

Also, during the night of November 14–15, 1938, the Jewess Anna Engelmann, née Sack, born May 29, 1869, in Bamberg, and residing at Otto St. 7, Bamberg, poisoned herself with veronal.

Both cases concern widows and were ruled suicides.

Looting, e.g., removal of objects for personal gain, did not occur during the protest riots.

During the protest riots 168 Jewish males were arrested and held at the county jail. Jewish females were not arrested.

After the separation of youths, Jews over 60 years of age, and the physically handicapped, 81 Jews were transferred to Dachau on the morning of Nov. 11, 1938. The separated Jews were released during the night of Nov. 10, 1938. Requests for the release of 25 Jews still held in the concentration camp at Dachau have so far been received.

2. To be routed, with enclosures, to the police commissioner of the city of Bamberg, for his information and with a request for transmittal to the office of the secret state police, Nuremberg, attention: Dr. Grafenbacher.

Bamberg, Nov., 26, 1938
Office of the State Police
Department P
[signed] Bezold

The fate of the Jews in "protective custody" in Dachau has
been well documented by the released prisoners. Their treatment did not differ from that of other concentration camp
inmates, with the only difference that they were Jews and had to
suffer for it constantly. Life became intolerable, aggravated by
situations such as standing for hours at attention during head
count, even in inclement weather; crowding of a great number
of people into small rooms; miserable food; and, above all, the
uncertain future. Fritz Grausmann (born 1892) still remembers
the shock one morning when the loudspeaker ordered the "Jew
Grausmann" to report to the gate. He was lucky. Through the
intervention of a business friend in the Netherlands (the Reich
valued the opportunity of export business), he was released.
However, before he left, a camp doctor examined him for signs
of abuse, such as welts, bruises, hemorrhages, and new scars. It
may well be imagined what would have happened if such traces
were found—the mildest consequence would have been a
delayed release.

The files of the Bamberg county court contain correspondence concerning the "Jewish farmer Max Sussmann of Aschbach." A victim of the "Revenge Operation," he wound up in
Dachau. The exchange of letters shows the fear of his relatives,
on the one hand, and, on the other, the cold bureaucratic
response and intimidation of the prisoner's family.

No. 60
I. Excerpts from the Weekly Report of the Burgwindheim
Constabulary Station, Jan. 7, 1939

In the course of measures taken against Jews, a Jewish farmer, Max Friedrich Sussmann, Aschbach, single, born Apr. 10, 1888, in Aschbach, was arrested on Nov. 10, 1938 and transferred to the county jail in Bamberg. It is assumed that Sussmann has been transferred to Dachau.

Of late, rumors have circulated in Aschbach that Sussmann is dead, killed by a bullet.

According to testimony by Sussmann's sister, Mina Bayer of Aschbach, nothing has been heard from him since his arrest. After inquiry at the county office in Bamberg, she received a reply stating that her brother was not registered as having arrived in Dachau and is not on the list of prisoners. Mina Baier [sic] is extremely worried about the fate of her brother. . . .

II. G.R. to: Burgwindheim Constabulary Station

Please note: After her inquiry of Nov. 28, 1938, the sister of inmate Max Sussmann, Mina Bayer of Aschbach, received notification that her brother was in the concentration camp at Dachau. Advise Jewess Mina Bayer to cease spreading untruthful rumors or be immediately put in protective custody.

Bamberg, January 13, 1939
      [signed]
      County Magistrate

[handwritten letter]

Jan. 15, 1939. To the County Magistrate District Bamberg.

We have notified the Jewess Mina Bayer of Aschbach, following the directives given by the county magistrate, Bamberg. She replied that there must be a misunderstanding. The information that her brother was not in Dachau did not originate in the county offices in Bamberg, but came directly from the office of the commander of the concentration camp at Dachau. In the future, she promised, she will adhere strictly to the rules of the law.

[signed]

To quell the rumor in Aschbach that Max Sussmann "was not alive," or, nearer to the truth, that he had been killed, pressure was put on the prisoner's sister. She was threatened with "protective custody" if she insisted on spreading "untruthful rumors." She promised that in the future she would adhere strictly to the rules of the law. Subsequent documents seem to be missing. Max Sussmann had disappeared into thin air. Obviously, additional inquiries brought no results until one day a notification arrived from the Dachau concentration camp that the missing Sussmann had died there. The last document in the file is a mimeographed form filled out by typewriter and sent from the Dachau camp administration to the Nuremberg-Fürth offices of the state police.

Dachau Concentration Camp March 16, 1939
Office of Prisoners' Property

to: Office of the State Police, Nuremberg-Fürth

List of property belonging to the Jew Sussmann, Max, born Sept. 10, 1889, deceased at the Dachau concentration camp, to be forwarded to you in the near future:

1 cap	2 shirts
1 coat	1 pair of underpants
1 jacket	1 pair of socks
1 vest	1 pair of shoes
1 pair of trousers	1 tie
1 sweater	1 collar
2 handkerchiefs	1 wallet

The property of the above-named inmate will be forwarded
to you by mail under separate cover.
Please sign enclosed receipt and return immediately to the
Office of Prisoner's Property, Dachau Concentration Camp.
Administrator of Prisoner's Property
[signed]
SS-Platoon Leader

According to several individuals who were prominent func-
tionaries in those days, some highly placed people in the government did not agree to the policies of November 9 and 10.
The operation, hastily ordered by Goebbels, ran counter to
Goering's effort to exploit the trade connections and wealth of
the Jews and triggered an unmistakable reaction in the foreign
press. Finally, it was a victory of the fanatics over those who
wanted to "solve the Jewish problem" but tried, at the same
time, to avoid the bad impression caused by the prevailing attitude toward Jews. However, Goering, one of the most outspoken critics of the "operation," was more motivated by his desire
for monetary gains. Utilization of Jewish capital was his guiding
principle.

On the morning of November 10, at 8:30 a.m., a coded radio
message arrived at Nuremberg-Fürth police headquarters,
marked secret and urgent:

Police Headquarters Nuremberg-Fürth
Nuremberg, Nov. 10, 1938

Police Communication Department
received: 0830, by: shuh
Secret! Urgent!

Radio Message
from: State Security Service, Berlin, No. 4, Nov. 10, 1938,
Time 0630
(coded) received Nov. 11, 1938 – No. 523

All-hands Order:

The fatal Jewish attack in Paris has triggered spontaneous demonstrations and actions throughout the German Reich against Jews, Jewish property, and Jewish synagogues. These demonstrations and actions are understandable. Certain guidelines regarding control and intervention will govern the police. The orders are:

1. Command headquarters of the uniformed police shall immediately contact the appropriate security agencies and stay in touch with the appropriate police departments and party offices, in order to be fully informed as to locations of demonstrations and actions.

2. The security police shall accompany these demonstrations and actions only with small plainclothes detachments and only to prevent possible looting. Uniformed police will only intervene in extreme emergencies. Arrests to be made by security police only.

3. Police offices must contact party offices immediately and must suppress arson attempts at all costs.

4. Unsecured destroyed shops, residences, synagogues, and Jewish businesses must be sealed and put under guard to avoid looting.

5. Reinforcement of police forces, if necessary, can be requested from the SS (active or reserve), as per order of H.H. [Heinrich Himmler].

6. Demonstrations and actions of extensive size must be reported to me at once.

Chief of Uniformed Police, Special Command
[signed] Daluege

Here the open question is: Is this a police force to call upon in time of need, the "friend and protector"? If orders to control and intervene must follow specific guidelines, all concepts of the task of a police force are violated. It is outrageous that the commander-in-chief of a police force, General Daluege, can call certain acts of violence "understandable." This is a revealing

insight into the internal workings of the police and the government, a relationship that made it possible for the Final Solution
to run a smooth course; an operation that could not have been
accomplished without the well-disciplined apparatus of those
institutions. Corruption crept in from time to time, reaching
into the higher ranks, but nothing in the "Old Austrian Style"
of *richten* [subtle bribery] could have resulted in the saving of
lives.

Here *richten* did not work; the Jews of Bamberg realized this
in the ensuing weeks. It was common knowledge that the Jews
were ordered to pay, as a penalty, the fine of one billion reichsmarks; anyone could read that in the official *Law Gazette*. What
was not known was the continuation of secret looting. Here and
there copies of decrees surface in the files; e.g., a letter stamped
"secret" from Gestapo headquarters in Berlin to all branch
offices of the state police:

Bamberg District Office
Copy of Copy No. 569
Secret!

Dr. Dr. Berlin Nue. 253 614 Nov. 26, 1938 14:45

To all State Police Offices.
          Urgent—Deliver at once.
Re: Procedures concerning property confiscated from Jews
during the protest riots.

The following procedures apply to the property of Jews confiscated during the protest riots, as outlined to me by Ministerial President General Field Marshal Goering, and are the
responsibility of the secret state police:
1. For property with known owners, the following applies:·
   (a) Securities, cash, jewelry, and objects of high value must
be securely stored and inventoried (listing owner, value, or

estimated value). These lists must be submitted marked with the file number appearing below. Securities, cash, and jewelry valued under 1,000 reichmarks must be returned to the owner (after signing of receipt). The same rule applies to household goods.

Property of higher value can be returned to the owner if proof of emigration in the near future can be documented. However, the appropriate office of the Finance Ministry must be contacted beforehand. Concerning objects of exceptionally high value, my decision must be obtained.

(b) Groceries and perishable goods valued at less than 1,000 reichmarks must be turned over to the local office of the Association for Retail Trade (after signing of receipts) and can be disposed of at their discretion. Exempted are groceries and perishables that can be certified as the property of Aryan owners. This property must be returned immediately to its rightful owners (after signing of receipts).

(c) Ready-made apparel must be returned to its owners, after consultation with the local office of the Association for Retail Trade.

2. For property without known owners, the following applies:

(a) Securities, cash, jewelry, and objects of high value (autos, furs, high-priced garments, etc.) must be turned over to the local office of the Finance Ministry (after signing of receipts).

(b) Groceries and perishables must be turned over to the appropriate office of the NSV [Nazi People's Welfare] (after signing of receipts), for distribution within their own jurisdiction.

(c) If objects listed under 2a are already in the hands of Nazi offices, they must immediately be handed over to the offices of the Finance Ministry.

A certain amount of property was confiscated by party members and their diverse organizations. However, the disposition of such property is the sole responsibility of the Gestapo. The Deputy Fuhrer issued a confidential ordinance (dated Nov. 23, 1938) ordering the surrender of such objects to the nearest office of the Gestapo at once. A similar ordinance has been issued by SS Headquarters and sent to all SS offices.

The National Association for Retail Trade will advise its local branch offices of further regulations. The Reich Finance Minister has distributed to his offices, for their information, a preliminary scheme, relating to above matters.

Criminal police national headquarters has circulated an advisory to its local offices, charging them with the retrieval of the stolen property and ordering them to assist the state police in all their activities.

Provisions have been made for all concerned government agencies to facilitate a speedy execution of the Minister President's orders. I anticipate that through the efficient cooperation of all offices we will achieve prompt results.

The administration will initiate rulings regarding compensation for Aryan establishments.

Gestapo Berlin II E 1 No. 1353/38 sign. Heydrich

The plan to rid the German economy of Jews progressed as anticipated. In November and December the liquidation of Jewish businesses skyrocketed. This was in accordance with the regulations issued after the November pogrom. The hour for Aryan take-over specialists had arrived. Jewish firms, such as banks or businesses in the hops trade, were conveyed into Aryan hands. Suddenly, influential party members were able to afford Jewish buildings on more than favorable terms. Many old Jewish firms, prominent in their fields, disappeared. Their owners emigrated or euphemistically "retired into private life."

The turn this "private life" occasionally took was illustrated by the complaints Bamberg's Jews made to the political police, as seen in a letter from Elsa Hess, dated November 28, 1938.

I hereby appeal to the Bamberg police bureau for help with this urgent request. Today, my landlord, Mr. F.L. of A— Street gave notice of eviction as of January 1, 1939. My husband, Wilhelm Hess, born July 12, 1881, and my son Artur Hess, born May 5, 1911, are in protective custody in Dachau. For obvious reasons, I am in complete physical and mental collapse and therefore unable to function normally. The main grounds for eviction was a denunciation, claiming my apartment was infested with bedbugs. Mr. L. hired an exterminator, Mr. Pflauger of Bamberg. He inspected my apartment thoroughly and professionally with the obvious results that it was free of vermin.

I beg the police department to prevail upon Mr. L. to postpone the eviction and wait until the return of my family from Dachau.

. . . .

For previously stated reasons [the family's planned emigration] and also because my son and my husband are the only ones able to handle the liquidation of the business, tax matters, and other regulations, I beg the police department with all my heart to release my husband and son from protective custody. They will then arrange for a speedy emigration. I myself am unable to attend to any matters; recent events have left me too weak and feeble. . . .

The "begging with all my heart" did no more than initiate four pages of correspondence with the political police, typical of the approach to requests of this sort. Department P of the Bamberg police bureau wrote to the commissioner on December 1, 1938: "The Bamberg passport office has no record of an application for emigration by Wilhelm Hess and his family. Therefore the release of the Jews Wilhelm and Artur Hess is not a priority matter."

On December 13, 1938, the commissioner again made inquiry to the political police regarding the "development of the emigration case of the Hess family." On December 20, the answer arrived:

> Records show the intention of the Hess family to emigrate to America. Affidavits have already been issued. The family has low numbers on the waiting list and expects to be called to Stuttgart at any moment. As of today, there is no record of a request by Mrs. Hess for emigration papers for herself and Wilhelm and Artur H.
>   Please note: Wilhelm Hess is over 50 years old.

On January 3, 1939, the commissioner reported the release of the "Jew Wilhelm Hess" from Dachau. However, his son Artur remained in custody. On January 7, the political police reported that at this point in time no application for emigration had been received. It is obvious that the shock of incarceration and the cumulative affect of all the other events made it difficult for the parents to give these matters their full attention. The final words in the file are dated January 13: "Release is not a priority matter."

A footnote: the family was not able to emigrate and was evacuated with the first transport to Riga in 1941.

Many similar letters as well as numerous passport applications have survived. In the weeks after the pogrom everybody wanted to emigrate, regardless of destination. People who previously had been hesitant about leaving tried to obtain visas and passports. Anything to get out, out of the Reich!

In many cases it was too late. The U.S. consulate in Stuttgart had a waiting list and issued consecutive numbers. The length of a wait for a visa was predictable—stretching into the year 1941, even 1942. Many became resigned, lost their illusions, and pursued emigration only half-heartedly. Others went in search of any solution, including "exotic" visas; the Dominican Republic and Shanghai (reachable only by the Trans-Siberian Railroad) became final destinations. Oral history interviews record the overly bureaucratic tendencies of foreign consulates, and this added to the difficulties. The attitude of the lower-ranking German personnel at the Stuttgart consulate was no different from that of their colleagues in German offices, especially when validating affidavits (the guarantee by a U.S. citizen to vouch for a prospective immigrant). The dotting of i's and crossing of t's, rude treatment, and long waits in the anterooms turned a visit to the consulate into torture. There was a pronounced feeling that the welcome mat was not out. As for the attitude of Germany's neighboring states, the less said the better.

The picture changed when one had good connections. A case in point is the release and emigration of Ernst Ludwig Silbermann and Hans Gerst of Bamberg. They were the son and son-in-law of the businessman William Silbermann, Promenade 2, and, like many other Bambergers, were taken into "protective custody" on November 10. On November 12, William Silbermann wrote to the administration of the Dachau concentration camp:

> The undersigned submits the following petition to the honorable administration: My son Ernst Silbermann and my son-in-law Hans Gerst of Bamberg are, as of the 11th of this month, in protective custody at your camp. Both are managers of my business, now in liquidation. I, the undersigned, am 75 years old and suffer from a heart ailment. Consequently, I am unable to pursue the liquidation. . . . I therefore humbly request the speedy release of said gentlemen in order to conduct the liquidation in an orderly fashion. I beg for favorable action upon my petition.

The answer of the "honorable administration" of K.Z. Dachau is not known. A copy of this letter went to the police commissioner, and he contacted the political police. Bezold replied that the release of inmates Ernst Silbermann and Hans

Gerst was not recommended. This was the status of the matter on November 21.

Three days later, the commissioner asked the Gestapo office in Nuremberg to release Silbermann and Gerst. Why the change of heart, why the extraordinary speed?

On November 23, Irma Gerst, wife of Hans Gerst, wrote to the commissioner:

> Enclosed is a letter from the Foreign Service of the United States of America, Stuttgart consulate (dated November 21), which I request to be returned to me. The letter states that my husband Hans Gerst and my brother Ernst Silbermann have permission to emigrate immediately. I request the release from protective custody of the above-mentioned, in order to expedite the departure.

In addition, on November 22, the consul general wrote directly to the political police. Nonetheless, the Gestapo took no action and and the entire matter seemed to be in limbo. On December 8, the consul general dispatched a letter to the next higher rung on the bureaucratic ladder: the state police in Nuremberg-Fürth. It is a remarkable document.

Stuttgart, December 8, 1938

To the Secret State Police
State Police Office Nuremberg-Fürth
Nuremberg

> I take the liberty to enclose a copy of my letter addressed to the Secret State Police, Bamberg (dated November 22) for your personal attention. I hope you will take into consideration the special interest shown by prominent people in the fate of Messrs. Hans Gerst and Ernst Silbermann.
>
> I take this opportunity to reiterate the fact that Hans Gerst and Ernst Ludwig Silbermann are relatives of very prominent

people in the United States. I again take the liberty to bring the case of the two above-mentioned gentlemen to your personal attention, in the hope that you will find it appropriate to release them, in order to facilitate their preparations for departure. I have received documents from the Assistant Secretary of State in Washington that leave no doubt that Hans Gerst and Ernst Ludwig Silbermann have permission to enter the United States, as soon as they reach their turn on the waiting list. I have good reasons to assume that a temporary stay in another country can be arranged until American entry visas can be issued. The file with the visa applications will be transferred to the consulate of the country of choice of the persons concerned.

All procedures can be expedited by the prompt release of Messrs. Hans Gerst and Ernst Ludwig Silbermann. In view of the prominent position of the relatives of these gentlemen in the United States, I express my hope that you will give the question of the release of both these gentlemen your favorable consideration. This will put them in a position to apply for a temporary stay in another country. I will be very much obliged if you would be kind enough to inform me of your decision in this matter.

> Sincerely yours,
> S. W. Honaker
> U.S. Consul General

In this letter the consul general pulled out all the stops, using all forms of persuasion. There is a very real story behind the effort of the State Department in Washington to help two "protective custody Jews" in Dachau. The prominent relatives of the two were Governor Herbert Lehman of New York and his family.

The correspondence initiated by one side (later branded as conspirators) triggered confusion on the other side, the bureaucracy. Already on December 13, an unnamed councillor of the

Bamberg county court hastened to inform the consulate as follows:

"In reply to your letter of Dec. 8, 1939, No. 81.11 SWH/GV, I am pleased to inform you that Mr. Hans Gerst and Mr. Ernst Silbermann of Bamberg were recently released from detention."

What civilized style! Suddenly a "protective custody Jew" turned into "Mister." The entire affair could be viewed as a comedy act, if it were not so tragic. Many other Jews, without the blessing of prominent relatives, were victims of bureaucratic chicanery on both sides and had to suffer to the bitter end. This incident points to the missed possibilities.

Finally, the consul general sent his thanks, polite and detached.

To the Hon. Commissioner of Bamberg

I am pleased to acknowledge the receipt of your letter of December 13, 1938, and take the opportunity to thank you for your cooperation in the matter of Messrs. Hans Gerst and Ernst Ludwig Silbermann.

Outside intervention led to release in a few other cases. Herbert Lindner was released after acquaintances in Strasbourg were able to convince the German consulate in Epinal to send a telegram to the police in Bamberg: "Due to intervention by prominent Alsatian firm must know date of release of manufacturer Herbert Lindner. Entry Luxembourg assured by French sources. Reply by return wire."

On December 12 the political police reported Herbert Lindner's release to the commissioner.

The deciding factor in the release of Fritz Grausmann, whose business was already in Aryan hands, was a telegram from the Heineken Brewery in Rotterdam, stating: "Payment for delivered hops is only possible in the presence of the former owner."

Moreover, the Aryan successor firm approached the Gestapo by submitting a letter, an act of considerable daring.

With these exceptions, all other efforts by relatives and friends to free the victims of "protective custody" were futile. The file contains many letters that brought no results. It was January, even February, before everybody was released from Dachau.

Note

The depiction of the November Pogrom in Bamberg relies on a very small source base. Descriptions of actual events are based on testimony at the trial of participants accused of setting the fire at the synagogue, held at the Bamberg County Court in 1946 (County Court Bamberg, KL's 15.46).

Files in the Bamberg county offices (the councillor acted as commissioner) document the problems of victims in regard to arrests, emigration, etc. (StAB K 5 n. 3148).

3

Prelude to the Final Solution: Identification and Exclusion

FOR A LONG TIME AFTER THE SEIZURE of power, anti-Jewish acts seemed to be aberrations, the by-products of a revolution. In fact, the emphasis of the drive to repress Jewish influence was shifted to legal proclamations. One gets the impression that the main objective was a limitation which would curtail Jewish predominance in many spheres of daily life, a notion which would be welcome to the nationalistic German petit bourgeoisie. Under this assumption even the Nuremberg Laws seemed acceptable, and what is more, many Jews themselves were of the opinion that the laws might well serve to quiet and clarify the atmosphere more than to aggravate the situation. Instead of arbitrary decrees by the party and the SA, the unequivocal rule of law would be applied. Even the limitless hate-mongering and rabble-rousing published in the *Stürmer* were tolerated on the assumption that they were a temporary affliction, manifestations of a sexually perverted and degenerate mind, almost ignored by the general public.

The laws enacted during those years showed clearly that the party and the government had no intention of being inhibited by moral principles and respect for civil rights in enforcing the disenfranchisement of the Jews, especially in the economic sphere. The implementation of the well-planned goal of "Aryanizing" the German economy started toward the end of 1937. Goering, as commissioner of the Four-Year Plan, seems to have been the driving force. Edicts required the registration of Jewish businesses and, above all, Jewish assets. The transfer of assets on emigrating to foreign countries was restricted and later completely prohibited. As early as July 16, 1933, an ordinance of the Reich Finance Ministry declared, on one hand, that Jewish emigration was a desirable goal, but, on the other hand, plundered the assets of the emigrants by levying a *Reichsfluchtsteuer* tax for "fleeing" the country. A Reich Commerce Ministry decree issued in June 1938 prohibited Jews from trading on the stock exchange. In July of the same year the Law to Restructure Trade in the German Reich prohibited Jews from engaging in a wide range of occupations. This edict concluded with a statement unprecedented for a civilized nation: "There will be no compensation for damages caused by the enforcement of this law."

In July 1938 further steps to be taken to identify, and thereby defame, German Jews were outlined in a bulletin entitled "Notification Regarding Issuance of Mandatory Identity Cards." An advisory circulated in 1939 does not quote the exact wording but conveys the intent and meaning of the law. Under the heading "System of Identification of Jews" these hints appear:

> Following the special measures introduced in the *Namensrecht* to facilitate identification of Jews, it is incumbent upon passport offices to take special care to exclude identification errors. . . . Passports for trips abroad are only valid if they carry a special identification stamp issued by the Reichsminister of the Interior (RMI), identifying the carrier as a Jew.

The identification stamp, in accordance with the Interior Ministry order, presumably introduced after consultation with the Swiss authorities, was a large yellow or red *J*. Nor was the

identification of Jews within the borders of the Reich overlooked.

> Similar to the stamp identifying Jews carrying a valid pass-
> port for trips abroad, an international I.D. card will show the
> same special stamp. . . . This card *can* be obtained by every
> German citizen over the age of 15 legally or permanently
> residing within Germany's borders. However, Jews who are
> German citizens *must* apply for this card.

The I.D. cards issued to Jews were stamped with the same *J*
found in passports.

> Jews over the age of 15 must be able to identify themselves,
> upon request by authorized persons, by producing their I.D.
> cards. In all transactions with government or party offices,
> such as petitions, submissions, or inquiries, Jews must men-
> tion their racial membership, the number of their I.D. card,
> and the name of the issuing office. On personal visits to the
> offices they must show their cards without being asked. Fail-
> ure to obey these orders will be punished by imprisonment,
> fine, or both.

The *Namensrecht* referred to earlier provided many opportunities for defamation. On August 17, 1938, a law was published
under the title "Regulations for Change of First Names and
Family Names." It ordered that Jewish citizens of the German
Reich assume first names from those listed in guidelines direct-
ing the choice of given names, issued by the Interior Ministry
of the Reich. Of course, the permitted names were not common
among the emancipated Jewish bourgeoisie in the 1920s and
1930s and would immediately brand the person with such a
name as a Jew, which was the intention in the first place. All
Jews whose first names were not found on this infamous list
were required, starting January 1, 1939, to add "Israel" or "Sara"
respectively to their full name. To add insult to injury, persons

affected by this law had to report the forcibly adopted name to the nearest registrar's office themselves. The threat of imprisonment for any failure to comply with this regulation typifies the mentality of the authors of this kind of legislation.

July 1938 brought the IV. Statute of Civil Law for German Citizens, resulting in the cancellation of the certification of Jewish physicians. Those receiving permission to treat "Jews exclusively" were stripped of the title "medical doctor" and designated "medical attendant."

The purpose of all these laws and many other regulations was obvious: to bring about the economic ruination and *Ausschalthung* ("elimination") of German Jewry, thrusting it into a position of diminished civil rights, perhaps with the ultimate goal of creating a criminal proletarian underclass, which would be prosecuted and finally eliminated as a matter of public cleansing, as an article in the *Schwarzes Korps* predicted.

Right after the November pogrom, an uncomprehending world was shown what else was possible in the realm of anti-Jewish measures. Between November 10, 1938 and August 24, 1939 a total of 229 laws and ordinances solely affecting Jews were enacted. Most of the regulations were defamatory, often with euphemistic titles, such as Directives for Jewish Businesses to Restore Streets to Their Normal Appearance. Translated, this meant that a Jewish business owner whose display windows were shattered had to repair damages to the exterior of his shop, caused by the SA or similar rabble, at his own cost and as soon as possible. The proceeds of insurance settlements were assigned to the Reich Treasury.

Some of the decrees of this period had shockingly outspoken titles, such as I. Law Concerning the Elimination of Jews from the German Economy. Others emphasized a benevolent innocence in their headings. Who would imagine that the V. Law Concerning Compliance with German Civic Order aided in the exclusion (the Nazi euphemism was *Ausschaltung*) of Jewish citizens from enjoying the fruits of their labors?

Drastic measures were taken, thereby threatening and profoundly impairing the life of each victim. Control of bank accounts was curtailed; the appearance of Jews in public places was restricted (the so-called *Judenbann*, a regression into medieval practices); drivers licenses were revoked; vehicle registrations were cancelled until finally the automobiles were "sold" to the Nazi Party at depressed prices; it is superfluous to mention the prohibition against a Jew requesting a hunting license or owning an ancestral estate; even "normal" German fellow citizens had to show proof of Aryan purity, back to January 1, 1800, to qualify.

Starting in November 1938, Jews were excluded from retail trade, the crafts and free enterprises. The *Entjudung der Deutschen Wirtschaft* ("removal of Jews from the German economy") reached its conclusion. To top it off, Germany's Jews were fined one billion reichsmarks as a sin offering for the hostile attitude of Jewry against the German people.

These were the conditions under which the Jews of Bamberg, and all others, had to live. There was no denying that the time for lulling oneself into a false sense of security had passed, and the politics of state and party struck a more aggressive course. The skeptics, whom some called pessimists, were proven right; the question was: What else could befall the Jewish community of Bamberg?

The next blow fell on April 30, 1939, in the form of a Law Concerning Rental Agreements with Jews, with its detailed regulations to be published soon afterwards. The gist of the law was that Jewish lessees were no longer protected under the rent laws if a gentile landlord certified that his Jewish tenant was able to find shelter elsewhere. The implementation directive states the meaning clearly: In the future, Jews would live in

Jewish-owned buildings, or to be more explicit, from now on Jews were not welcome in Aryan buildings. A clause appended to the law tried to give a human face to the order: Eviction of Jews by force was only to take place when necessary.

By the spring of 1939 the concentration of Jews in a handful of buildings was very obvious. The *Bamberger Volksblatt* had already announced the imminent enforcement of the *Entjudung*, reporting:

> Jews will disappear from Aryan neighborhoods. The repression of Jews will be noticeable in other ways. For example, it is now possible to exclude Jews from tenant associations. The results will be clear: Jews will have to leave the predominantly Aryan neighborhoods in the near future. If it should become apparent that not enough apartments are available, the remaining propertied Jewish families will have to open their residences, villas, and even their mansions to their racial comrades.

Details of the evictions of Jews in Bamberg are not known; how often the application of force became necessary is also an unknown matter. However, the result reveals itself through a comparison of the last prewar population directory with the list of addresses of deportees in 1941–42. Some buildings became distinct *Judenhäuser*, such as the house at Sophien (today Willy-Lessing) Street 7, where, at the end of 1939, many "resettled" Jewish families resided. The path from the residence of families in high social and economic positions to the shelter of a deprived underclass is more than evident.

In 1941, at the time of the first deportations, a substantial number of houses with a majority of Jewish residents, the so-called *Judenhäuser*, existed. Many of the tenants had been forced from their former apartments during the enforcement of the *Entjudung* laws in the fall of 1938. These were the addresses:

Kessler Street 18
Zinkenwörth 17 (the White Dove Inn)
Heinrichsdamm 1
Hain Street 4a
Sophien Street 7
Hauptwach Street 14
Luitpold Street 48
Zinkenwörth 5
Herzog-Max Street 3
Friedrich Street 8
Franz-Ludwig Street 26

The lively pace at which the Jewish populace of Bamberg fulfilled its obligation to move is evidenced by the index cards listing addresses and family groups in the files of the Bamberg residential registry. For example, in October 1939 alone, the above-mentioned house at Sophien Street 7, property of the estate of the manufacturer Max Kupfer, was the refuge of three Jewish families. A move from well-appointed middle-class apartments to much smaller quarters was, without doubt, the result of the announced and desired disappearance of Jews from Aryan neighborhoods.

The irony was that many Jews relocating under the new laws by no means came from Aryan neighborhoods, but from streets where well-to-do Jewish citizens had lived since the nineteenth century.

The story behind the evictions becomes clearer when one reads a document from Forchheim/Upper Franconia (no comparable papers surfaced in Bamberg). This letter, dating from 1941, originated at the Altstadt and Bahnhof local branches of the Nazi Party in Forchheim, and was addressed to the mayor of the town:

Just as irritating [referring to the actions of farmers in the district who occasionally slipped food to Forchheim's Jews] is the intolerable situation that, as of today, Jewish parasites still live at Paradeplatz 4. This building fronts on the parade grounds of the party and its affiliated organizations, and furthermore stands on the extension of the main street of our town, Adolf-Hitler Street. The final eviction of Jews residing in this building, or any other in the city's center, is a matter of utmost urgency, in order to avoid further spread of a festering rage among our population. We refrain from depicting a reversed situation, a Jewish town of 11,000 parasites and 10 Germans among them and what the Jewish parasites would have done. We beg you to take appropriate measures to eliminate these intolerable conditions now. Furthermore, we have been informed of the establishment of headquarters in Forchheim of a company of Hitler Youth and a troop of BDM [Bund Deutscher Mädchen (Union of German Girls)]. The leadership of these organizations is in dire need of sufficient space. The shortage of apartments within the city precludes the procurement of suitable accommodations. In the interest of disciplined leadership and to avoid jeopardizing the politically significant formation of these youth groups, we request that special measures be taken. We propose the relocation of all the Jewish families now residing at Paradeplatz 4 in Forchheim to empty barracks, formerly used as living quarters. What was acceptable to our fellow Germans should, without doubt, be acceptable to Jews.

The writer's words reflect his state of mind. He uses the jargon of the exterminator's trade, speaking of the fight against infestation by vermin.

Letters in this vein could well have been used in Bamberg's effort to speed up the *Entjudung* of neighborhoods. All the Jews living in Bamberg during those years and the victims of the chicanery of *Entjudung* of apartments must have had neighbors and fellow tenants. Why was it, when I questioned the latter, that hardly anybody could remember what was played out in their immediate vicinity?

In the months preceding the outbreak of World War II, it became painfully clear that worse than the expulsion from German society was in store for the Jews. Hitler's threats became more outspoken. Those who had hesitated in the past were now frantically looking for an opportunity to emigrate. The owner of a hardware store was urged by his employees to leave the country, even though it was against his own inclination. He was of the opinion that matters could not get much worse, and as long as he was able to stroll in the Hain (a park), he was content. Some were convinced that their status as war veterans and war invalids would protect them "from the worst." Of course nobody could imagine what the "worst" was going to be. Why can't we understand this attitude? Here was Bamberg, the city of one's residence for many decades, where every paving block was known, where one had gotten married and raised children; and there, a far-off, strange country. Here, one was among people whose language one understood, to whom—some still believed—one was able to speak, in spite of the fact that when encountered, they did not greet you and even looked away; and over there, people who regarded you as a an undesirable alien, a refugee, if they consented to let you enter in the first place.

This was the fate of the disabled war veteran Albert Walter of Luitpold Street 26, second floor—and many, many others. Finally, when they realized under the hail of laws and decrees that all this was directed against them personally, so to speak, it was in most cases too late to succeed in making arrangements for emigration.

Nazi anti-Semitism was a curious mixture of a pseudoscientific theory of race, an obtuse superiority complex of supermen, and a calculating desire for personal gain. The pronouncements of leading Nazis were often obscure and cloudy, and, as was frequently the case with Hitler's speeches, of ominous consequences. The emotional outbursts aroused grave apprehension, but were often weakened and watered down.

The official goal regarding the Jewish question was already formulated in the 25-point platform of the Nazi Party published on February 24, 1920:

4. To be a citizen of the state one must be a *Volksgenosse* [fellow countryman]; a *Volksgenosse* is a person of German blood, regardless of religion. Hence, no Jew can be a *Volksgenosse.*

5. Non-citizens are allowed to live in Germany as guests only, and are regulated by special laws applicable to foreigners.

At first sight this was a relatively benign formulation of a political statement. German citizens with nationalist tendencies not only accepted these claims, but found them to represent a desirable aim: Germany for the Germans. The methods applied at the dawn of National Socialism foreshadowed their frequent and ready use in later years. The segregation of a certain section of the population with the aid of a frivolous pretext: pseudoscientific criteria to "prove" that racial characteristics separate certain people from the majority of the nation. These invented differences of race and mentality, which would not stand up under rational scrutiny, were used to formulate special laws and then force them on this particular group under the guise of a "special status in the structure of the German nation." These special laws alone defined the minority group. The study of Nazi propaganda invariably leads to this conclusion. In this atmosphere it is no aberration that somebody like Walter Busch was able to publish in the semiofficial *Deutsche Justiz* in 1936: "National Socialism recognizes that the Jew is not a human being. He is a manifestation of decay."

It is possible that under such conditions fantasies of eliminating the Jew started to take hold. Evidence of these fantasies, early on expressed by Hitler in the terminology of an exterminator, can be found in the first edition of *Mein Kampf.* He wrote:

> If only during the war, from the very start, we had exposed twelve or fifteen thousand of those Hebrews, the corrupters of our nation, to a dose of poison gas, the same gas endured on the battlefield by hundreds of thousands of our best German soldiers in all fields, of all classes, then the sacrifice of millions at the front would not have been in vain.

The anti-Semitism of the 1930s had two parallel factions. On the one hand, a majority of the nation approved the forcing back of Jewish influence; on the other hand, a small group, with Hitler as whip and spokesman, gained in influence in the Nazi state and advocated a Final Solution through physical extermination.

It was disastrous that both factions had at their service the well-oiled machinery of government and a perfect bureaucracy, expected to function well. This apparatus executed to the satisfaction of all the task of enforcing increasingly stringent measures, whether the statutory confiscation of Jewish assets or total annihilation; both were viewed as administrative functions, and moral scruples could be excluded.

The Ressource in Hain Street, which was an exclusive membership club for the Jews of Bamberg.

April 1, 1933. Boycott of Jewish stores. Picket line of S.A. men in front of Jewish textile store on Hauptwach Street.

Interior of Bamberg synagogue. East view toward the holy ark.

Willy Lessing, Kommerzienrat, patron and trustee of the congregation. He died in January, 1939 as a result of severe beatings during the pogrom of the night of November 9, 1938.

November 10, 1938. Jews of Bamberg on the way to jail, accompanied by police and S.A.

November 10, 1938. The synagogue, covered with anti-Jewish graffiti, on the morning after the fire.

March 1939. Demolition of the ruins of the synagogue.

The synagogue disappears from the panorama of the city. Complete removal of the ruins followed the conflagration.

After the demolition of the synagogue, a celebration on top of the rubble. District leader Zahneisen addresses Bamberg's "dignitaries."

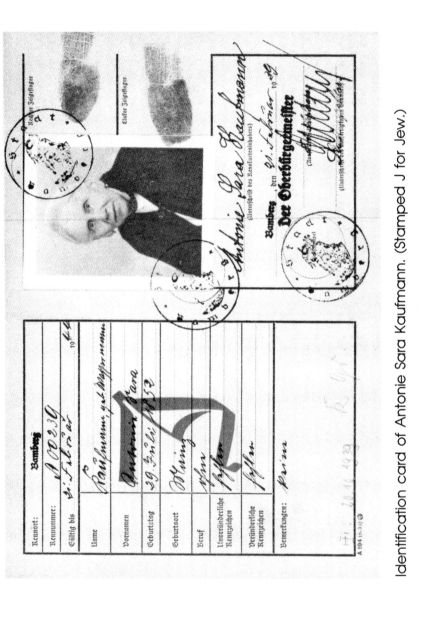

Identification card of Antonie Sara Kaufmann. (Stamped J for Jew.)

4

Jewish Life at the Beginning of the War

AT THE BEGINNING OF 1939, no one could or would have imagined that the curtailment and debasement of Jews in public by means of restrictions on their way of life would one day lead to officially sanctioned and executed annihilation. Bamberg's Jews were well aware that they faced hard times, but they hoped, even under the restrictions, to remain Jews and to be able to live a Jewish life.

After long negotiations and many difficulties, before the expropriations, an agreement was reached with the authorities to prevent the expropriation of the social hall of the White Dove Inn which was supposed to be converted into a grain storage facility. Eventually, the frightened and considerably shrunken congregation was allowed use of the same location for prayer services, a pitiful shelter after the loss of a beautiful big synagogue. Nevertheless, religious life took on a semblance of order, as can be seen from the Prayer Schedule of the Hebrew Congregation of Bamberg for April, May, and June of 1939, which has survived. After his release from Dachau, Rabbi Dr. Max Katten emigrated to England. Occasionally, Dr. Behrend of Fürth officiated at services and religious ceremonies. The reaction in Bamberg was similar to that in many other places. Persecution and oppression led to stronger adherence to the common faith.

On February 21, 1939, it was once more Hermann Goering, commissioner of the Four-Year Plan, who imposed an arbitrary confiscation through the III. Regulations Concerning the Registration of Jewish Assets. All Jews, except citizens of foreign countries, had to surrender all objects in their possession made of gold, silver, or platinum, as well as precious stones and pearls, at officially designated purchase agencies, within two weeks. The victims, of course, had to accept the offer of the state's purchasing agent; in other words, objects made of precious metals or precious stones, the personal property of the owners, had to be surrendered for an insufficient compensation, and furthermore, the proceeds were subject to the law restricting access to Jewish assets!

In Bamberg, without doubt, this matter was interpreted as intended: the confiscation of personal property. On March 10, 1939, a bulletin was sent to all members of the Jewish community:

> To the members of our community
> Re: Surrender of jewelry and objects of precious metal by Jews
>
> It is strongly advised not to wait till the last day of the month but to proceed with the delivery to the municipal lending institution; otherwise extreme difficulties may be expected. We recommend to our members not to postpone registration by phone, but to call there as soon as the objects subject to surrender are collected and assembled. This will forestall constant complaints in the coming weeks of failure to fulfill the obligation of surrendering these objects in Bamberg. This warning is given to members of our community in their own interest.
>
> After March 22, the city loan institution will give preference to out-of-town applicants over citizens of Bamberg.

This can have dire consequences, especially in view of the increase in the number of out-of-towners.

Administration of the Jewish Community
of Bamberg
Dr. Martin Israel Morgenroth

What were the feared "extreme difficulties"? We can only suspect: arrest and transfer to Dachau.

On March 24, 1939, an additional bulletin was delivered to the members of the community, thereby illustrating the persistent and forceful effort to rid the Jews of the last remnants of their property for the profit of the Reich.

To the members of our community
Re: Surrender of jewelry and precious metals

1. Coin collections.
   We direct attention to the obligation to follow these regulations. Valuable coin collections, systematically catalogued by numismatic rules and kept in collectors' boxes and cases, must be surrendered as a whole, including the containers. The removal of the collection from its containers is prohibited. Permits and releases issued by the Reichsbank must be submitted by the owner to the purchasing agent when surrendering the coins.
2. Postponement of the surrender of jewelry and precious metals past the Mar. 31, 1939 deadline is out of the question, as well as any other dispensations, as was pointed out in previous notices.
3. Those on the verge of emigration are prohibited from taking additional objects now available due to recent release from confiscation. Any permits concerning foreign exchange and other dispensations issued by the Reichsbank are now null and void.

The language here discloses a marked trend, symptomatic of the horrible course of the Final Solution. Jewish organizations had received a charter from the Reichsverband der Juden in Deutschland (Federation of Jews in the German Reich) in July 1938. Recorded history shows that after the November pogrom, the independence of Jewish organizations diminished rapidly and the Gestapo clearly interfered in their inner workings. The autonomy of the Jewish religious communities was gone. They were used exclusively as agencies of the Reichsvereinigung der Juden, which served as the mouthpiece of the Gestapo, delivering messages to the members of the comunity. Without putting a fine point on it, it was in this way that the Gestapo worked its way directly into the individual religious communities. We will expand on this at a later point.

Testimony by an official of the city's finance bureau, given after the war during a restitution trial, described the activities of the municipal pawnshop. Similar scenes were depicted by Mr. L., a former appraiser and auctioneer for the city of Bamberg: One day, toward the end of 1939, a Jewish woman appeared with a basket full of silverware. The following days other Jewish Bambergers showed up, and about the same time a directive from the "higher authorities" was received, stating that all Jews wishing to emigrate must surrender their gold and silver objects to the purchasing agency. The repeated pressure by the communal administration, admonishing members to comply strictly with the regulations concerning the surrender, showed results. This is mirrored in the testimony of the official:

> Toward the end of the deadline, the pawnshop was over-whelmed by the stream of clients. . . . Mr. N. was the only person to assist me. . . . In September 1939, we began to open each and every package, in order to appraise the contents according to the official guidelines. It became apparent that many Jews included objects that were not covered by the regulations, such as silver-plated objects. Some packages contained, among other things, shirt and blouse buttons with a

glimmer of gold. They were included because of the fear of risking prosecution.

We learn about the value assigned to objects:

> A watch with gold casing and a cover with spring release was appraised for the value of the gold only. A standard man's pocket watch was entered for between 4.0 and 5.0 reichmarks. According to the regulations, the movement of the watch was not included in the estimate.

One of the Third Reich's most ostentatious propaganda achievements—meant to demonstrate the nation's community spirit—was the *Opfersonntag* ("Self-Sacrifice Sunday"), also known as *Eintopfsonntag* ("One-Course Meal Sunday"). Once a month, German families were called upon to restrict the customary Sunday meal to one simple dish and donate the savings to the NSV [People's Welfare Office of the Nazi Party]. A side effect of this custom was the ample opportunity given to local leaders (and heads of women's organizations, often the fanatical priestesses of Hitlerism in everyday life) to conduct inspection visits and stick their noses into everybody's pots. Nonparticipation in the *Eintopf* was considered a form of treason.

The *Eintopf* Sunday was, to some extent, a sign of the times and was also adopted by the Jews of Bamberg. The community designated one Sunday a month as *Eintopf* Sunday, and March 19, 1939 was one of these. Members were requested to make contributions to the community's welfare committee. An appeal dated March 14, 1939 featured a calendar with March 19 circled and the words: "Attention! Last *Eintopf!* Double your Donation!" Also enclosed was an appeal for the *Pfundspende* (the donation of at least one pound of nonperishable groceries) and a request to bring used clothing to the community storeroom. All this may give the impression of imitative toadying, but in reality it reflected the grave economic situation of many of the community's members. Pleas for aid and contributions for many causes became routine.

The 1939 celebration of the High Holidays, New Year and the Day of Atonement, took place right after the start of the war. Most of the Jews remaining in Bamberg realized that emigration was difficult, if not impossible, and that life would now take a turn for the worse. The newsletters issued by the community leave no doubt. On August 28, shortly before the invasion of Poland, this advisory was distributed:

> To the members of our community!
> 1. This request is made in the interest of all of us. Taking into account the grave situation, we strongly urge you to refrain from all ostentatious and objectionable behavior in the streets (congregating in groups and loud talk, especially before and after prayer services) and to avoid any noisy conversations in the garden of the White Dove that could cause offense to the neighbors.
> 2. Due to the heavy workload caused by urgent government requirements, the community office will be closed to the public today, Monday, August 28, 1939, in order to give us time to complete all the paperwork.
> Administration of the Jewish Community
> of Bamberg
> as per Dr. Ludwig Israel Oster

"Congregating in groups" and" noisy conversations" on the streets, as well as in the garden of the White Dove, could "cause offense" and make "bad blood." One does not need much empathy to imagine the atmosphere in the neighborhoods where Bamberg's Jews resided during the first days of World War II. The community administration apparently did not believe that the first warning was strong enough and circulated a second, stronger one, on September 4, appealing to the members' good upbringing and conscience.

Administration of the Jewish Community
Bamberg

Bamberg, September 4, 1939

To all the members of our community!

In spite of repeated strong warnings to show utmost restraint during these grave days, it has come to our attention that some of our members do not seem to comprehend the demands of the times.

Again, we emphatically demand adherence to the following rules: No unnecessary lingering in the streets—except for needed purchases or similarly urgent business—particularly no idle loitering, or worse, the congregating of two or more persons for conversations in the open streets or squares of the city (this includes sitting on benches).

At all times avoid pushing and loud behavior while shopping or dealing with official agencies. To the contrary, show in all cases the utmost restraint and a calm, dignified demeanor. Not one single individual dare jeopardize our entire community by unseemly and objectionable behavior. Each and every one is doubly responsible to all of us.

We appeal to the sense of responsibility of all the members of our community.

We declare explicitly that persons lacking in discipline and understanding, who, in spite of urgent warnings, disregard our requests, and who, by irresponsible behavior, give grounds for public and official complaints, will be denied, without leniency, the support of the community. The common good means more to us than any individual's inconsiderateness, obstinacy, and lack of a sense of solidarity.

We ask the support of all the responsible members of our community to help us prevent any incidents that could result in complaints from the general public. We recommend taking the initiative and interfering, if necessary, right then and there, in an unobtrusive, but decisive manner.

We are confident that our recent warnings and requests are fully understood by all the members of our community and will result in honest and willing cooperation with our community as a whole, without the shirking of responsibility.

Jewish Community of Bamberg
as per Dr. Ludwig Israel Oster

What looks at first sight like a warning to tramps and loiterers was, in all seriousness, directed at a segment of the population that only recently had been regarded as the cream of Bamberg society. It is not known whether these suggestions, singling out individuals who did not understand the demands of the times, were the result of actual incidents, but it must be kept in mind that during the first days of the war the situation was highly emotional. Trifling matters, which in normal times would have been silently dismissed with a shrug of the shoulders, could trigger grave consequences and turn into cases of great importance. Furthermore, the press was full of accusations, informing everyone where to put the real blame for the outbreak of the war: on the Jews, of course. The first commandment of civil duty for Jews was not only quiet behavior but also discretion and invisibility. The exceptionally strong and urgent wording of these bulletins has to be read in this context: absolutely no provocations.

One quite naturally asks, what is the story behind all these inferences? Sufficient evidence does not exist, either from contemporary documents or police files. On the other hand, it is hard to believe that in September of 1939, after the November pogrom and the hail of anti-Jewish laws and decrees, anybody might misread the signs of the times and behave insolently in public places, whatever this meant. Documents from Baden [a state in southwestern Germany] lead to the conclusion that in the first weeks of World War II, in certain locations, the mere appearance of a Jew in public was considered an affront, and official regulations, mostly curfews for Jews, were soon instituted. In this light, the documents that survived in Bamberg must be viewed as preventive measures, intended to give the the Jewish communal administration an opportunity to demonstrate its respect for law and order by using certain words in its notices. These communications had to be approved by the local branch of the Gestapo, of course. Presumably, warnings of this kind would prevent more drastic steps by the police. The position of the Jewish communal administration was difficult enough in any case. On one hand, it was the official representative of Bamberg Jewry; on the other hand, as an agency of the Reichsvertretung (the umbrella organization of Jews in the Reich, supervised by the Gestapo), it was obligated to cooperate with the police, now in charge of enforcement of the laws concerning Jews. How much input the Gestapo had in the wording of the communications issued by the community is unknown. In most cases official pronouncements were identified as such.

On September 1, the day the German army invaded Poland at dawn, new regulations against Jews were issued.

> The Reichsführer of the SS and Commander-in-Chief of the German Police Forces orders the following:
>
> 1. Jewish communities are ordered to build their own air raid shelters.
> 2. The Jewish community will make it known that Jews are forbidden to be out after 8:00 p.m.
>   I urge the Jewish communal administration and persons in charge of Jewish religious institutions to announce the above regulations immediately.
>   According to the express order of the Reichsführer SS, any mention of the above decrees in newspapers or official

publications is prohibited.

In this case, as in many others, the organs of the Jewish community had to act as middlemen for the authorities in charge of the "Jewish Question"; even more so because of the reluctance to announce officially the discriminatory restrictions on free movement. This resulted in an advisory notice circulated among the members of the Jewish community of Bamberg, headed:

> Important notice to the members of our community!
> Re: Curfew
>
> According to regulations issued by the highest police authorities, it is strictly prohibited to be on the streets after 8:00 p.m. Violators will be punished immediately. (Exemptions are only given in the most urgent cases, such as summoning a doctor for a seriously sick person, if no phone is available, the outbreak of a fire, or similar situations. In such cases, the reason for the emergency must be announced immediately when encountering patrols checking the streets.)

To avoid causing a bad impression abroad, the German press was asked to soft-pedal the news about the Jewish curfew with threadbare explanations, such as occurrences of molestation of Aryan women by Jews during the blackout.

This scenario was played out against an atmosphere of insecurity and anxiety caused by the sudden outbreak of war that caught many by surprise. The demonstrations of patriotic fervor of the year 1914 were lacking. Observers and diarists describing those days agree unanimously that the mood of the population was depressed and somber. The *Bulletin of Internal Affairs of the Security Service*, usually presenting a relatively unretouched picture of the mood in the Reich, also had to report the lack of enthusiasm for war among the populace. Taking this into consideration, the leadership refrained from going public with additional anti-Jewish measures. The fiasco of November 1938 was still clear in their minds; in spite of intensive preparations by the propaganda machinery, the broad masses had not been whipped into a popular uprising against the Jews. Hitler had declared, for the longest time, that the Final Solution of the Jewish Question was an absolute must in the event of a new war; but given the prevailing circumstances and in order to avoid a bad impression abroad, it had to be achieved under the cover of secrecy. As a matter of fact, Jew-baiting was relegated to the back pages of the newspapers. The target for hatred was not the individual Jew but an abstract concept called World Jewry. The press ceased to publish and comment on what official language termed "measures against Jews." The headquarters of the Reich Security Service, via the Gestapo, quietly and stealthily used the Jewish community administrations as conduits and held them responsible for dissemination and compliance.

Following is the scenario played out on the publication of Notice II B 4 - 982/39 J, issued by the headquarters of the Reich Security Service on September 20, 1939. The regulation prohibited German Jews and Jews without nationality (*staatenlos*) from listening to broadcasts in their homes. Radios owned by Jews had to be surrendered—without compensation, of course—"to be utilized by the German authorities for more useful purposes in the service of the nation." This was followed by: "This order must be executed uniformly on September 23, 1939." September 23 that year happened to be Yom Kippur, the Day of Atonement. We can assume that the form and haste employed in issuing this regulation was intended to forestall any undue interest among the general public. And so it became the burden of the officers of the Jewish community to notify their members of this new turn of the screw.

The bulletin issued by the Bamberg Jewish community (dated September 25) has survived. Obviously, the deadline for the uniform execution on September 23 had passed. This is the text of the notification:

> Re: Radio sets
>
> In accordance with orders from the authorities, we again urgently request that all the members of our community surrender their radio sets regardless of their condition (even if they are not in working order) by 6:00 p.m. tonight (Monday evening) at the latest, to the local office of the political police. We explicitly draw your attention to the severe punishment prescribed for willfully concealing or retaining any radio set. Only sets which have passed customs inspection prior to emigration are exempted from confiscation; but even in these cases it is advisable to notify the political police.

There was no good reason for the confiscation of radio sets. The pretense was the assumption that ability to receive broadcasts from abroad would contribute to the dissemination of rumors and open the door to espionage. The real reason might have been an easy opportunity to harass and humiliate the Jews; to push them into a position of diminished rights (culminating in no rights whatsoever). Nothing is known about the surrender of radio sets in Bamberg, since the press, as instructed, refrained from reporting on matters of this kind. Stuttgart was able to add additional harassment to the regulation: surrender by the owner personally (no proxy) and only at one receiving depot. The trek through the city turned into a running of the gauntlet. In Bamberg, too, the walk to the political police (this former designation remained in common use) at the old town hall was no pleasure trip. To make Yom Kippur the day of the surrender was a tortment of a special kind which assaulted a deep religious feeling of every observant Jew.

Religious feelings were taxed even more, as can be deduced from a bulletin of the Jewish community regarding the High Holidays. The New Year fell on September 14th and 15th, Yom

Kippur on the 23rd, coinciding with the *Blitzsieg* ("lightning victory") in Poland, just as the doubts of the majority about the government's war policies turned into a giddy victory celebration. This explains the strong wish of the Jewish communal administration that community members not attract attention.

Bamberg, September 11, 1939

Zinkenworth 17, I

To the members of our community!

I. Re: Prayer services on the High Holidays.

1. With the permission of the authorities, services will be held at the following hours, albeit in reduced form due to prevailing conditions. . . .

2. For your special attention: We repeat the urgent request that all members of our community refrain from inappropriate behavior on the way to and from the services, to avoid jeopardizing the opportunity given us by the authorities to conduct services:

a. No more than two persons shall walk together and any congregating of larger groups must be avoided.

b. It should be self-evident that everybody should refrain from wearing ostentatious clothing.

c. Also desist from the following: any kind of New Year's congratulations in the street; especially shouting New Year's greetings in a loud voice; avoid under any circumstances open encounters in the street for the above purposes.

d. It is urgently requested to maintain quiet in front of the prayer hall, especially after the conclusion of the services; to refrain from loud conversations and to follow the directions given by the appointed ushers without question.

e. . . .

f. Only strict discipline and everybody's submission to the rules, as dictated by the conditions of our times, will allow us to hold prayer services without obstacles on the High Holidays and perhaps again on other holidays and on Saturdays.

We appeal again to the sense of responsibility of each and every person in our community, man or woman, old or young!

II. . . .

III. . . .

Administration of the Jewish Community in Bamberg
as per Dr. Ludwig Israel Oster

The administration sends best wishes to all members of our community, *l'schono tauwo!* ["to a good year"].

The preceding document leads to the conclusion that conducting Jewish prayer services was prohibited in most cases. This might have been a by-product of the restrictions on free movement imposed on Jews at the beginning of September. The communal administration must have understood that the permission granted for the High Holidays was an exception. Who issued this permit cannot be learned from the surviving documents. Presumably it was the local branch of Gestapo headquarters in Nuremberg that gave permission to hold the prayer services after weighing the local circumstances. There are known cases where such a permit was withheld under very weak pretexts, such as fear for the security of the Jewish members of the community, a veiled hint of threats by local SA circles.

The Jews became the official enemy of the entire police apparatus of the Greater German Reich when jurisdiction over the Jewish Question was transferred from party offices to police bureaus and thereby from the realm of caprice to the world of law and order. What seems at first to be objectification was in reality a radicalization of the Jewish Question. Technocratic punctiliousness and familiarity with routine took over. Sheer hatred was replaced by perfection and a complete grasp of the task.

The German police force in those days was a curious creature, whose structure was very unclear, due to the parallel functions of a "traditional" police force on one hand and the branches of the SS on the other. In 1940, Werner Best wrote a book, *The German Police*, that tried to make the difficult structure a little more transparent: "The overall leadership of police forces in the entire Reich is in the hands of the Reichsführer SS and Commander-in-Chief of the German police; responsibility for specific areas has been given to the higher echelons of the SS and police."

The double-track of the police chain of command emerges clearly: the Commander-in-Chief of the police forces and the Reichsführer SS are one and the same person, Heinrich Himmler, who in 1943 also took over as Reichsminister of the Interior and thereby became his own boss. Parallel to the Gestapo, the secret state police (a "traditional" branch of any police force), was the Sicherheitsdienst (Security Service), known as the SD, in most cases run by the identical personnel. According to Best, "Even though the SD was a branch of the SS and therefore of the Nazi Party, it was empowered to aid the police in the task of maintaining security." The SD had its own table of organization with SD sectors and SD local branches parallel to the state police. The highest authority in the SD was the Reichssicherheitshauptamt (Reich Security Headquarters), subdivided into six sections. Section IV was responsible for the Jewish Question under the title *Gegnerbekämpfung* ("control of enemy activities"). The office directly responsible for Bamberg's Jews was the Gestapo branch in Bamberg, located in the old town hall. This office was formerly known as the political police and was the bailiwick of Commissioner of Criminal Police Bezold, a man who faithfully served both the Republic and the Third Reich; in other words, the type of bureaucrat who gives the impression of a solid and incorruptible worker.

Nevertheless, Karl Bezold showed the traits of a dual personality. Several Bamberg Jews who were able to emigrate reported that he personally tried to smooth their way to emigration whenever possible; for example, by circumventing bureaucratic measures or softening their impact. (On this man's inconsistent behavior see note 2, below.)

The political police (despite the new designation in 1933, this name remained in use in Bamberg) mirrored the picture of contradictions found in many agencies of the Third Reich. Yet to Bamberg's Jews it was the ultimate authority, unpredictable and feared. Community bulletins referred to it as the *Behörde* ("authorities"), a nameless, impersonal calamity. The relationship of Bamberg's Jews with the government had obviously shrunk to their contacts with the almighty political police.

In the fall of the year 1939, Bamberg's Jews were visited by a misfortune of a different sort. In a short span of time Julius Wassermann and Martin Morgenroth died. The deaths of these competent jurists must have been an irreplaceable loss. New elections for the executive board became necessary, a portentous undertaking in these troubled times. In spite of the complete lack of source material, it is obvious that the elections took place under the control of the Gestapo. It must have been difficult to find candidates who enjoyed the trust of the community members and, at the same time, were acceptable to the "authorities." We learn of the election results in a bulletin of the Jewish community, dated October 26, 1939: chairman of the executive board, Dr. Siegmund Bauchwitz; first vice-chairman, Sally Brandes; second vice-chairman: Josef Hessberg. We do not know who the other candidates were, who was unacceptable to the "authorities," and why Dr. Bauchwitz was the ultimate winner. He was a physician, renowned and beloved, now reduced to functioning as the Jewish medical attendant; a man who, when encountering colleagues on Langen Street, fearfully crossed the street to avoid compromising them by his mere presence.

The life of a Jewish medical attendant is well documented in the files of the District Office of Public Health, which survived the war.

As early as November 17, 1938, a bulletin of the Reichsärzteführer (head of the Reich Medical Association) determined that the regulations against Jewish physicians, such as the revocation of licenses and the prohibition to practice, were too severe. "It can hardly be our goal to fill the waiting rooms of German physicians with Jews. We have already received complaints from doctors in different localities stating that their waiting rooms are overrun by Jews."

Naturally, this was an undesirable side-effect, and the Medical Association was stranded between Scylla and Charybdis. "Physicians, as well as gentile patients, are rightfully offended." "Rightfully," after they themselves created the situation, in order to fulfill the mandate of *Entjudung*? This led some physicians to post notices in their waiting rooms, advising, JEWS NOT TO BE TREATED HERE. This kind of behavior caused the head of the Medical Association to examine his moral conscience; after all, even a true Nazi had to adhere to the ethics of his profession! The law creating "Jewish medical attendants"—the word "doctor" was still taboo in this context—was interpreted a little more generously. It was admitted, with great regret: "There is no prohibition under the law for Jewish attendants to retain the title 'Dr.', be it in the form of 'Dr.', 'Dr.med.', or 'Professor', and we are unable to restrict the use of the title. On the other hand, the designation 'physician' is prohibited, even in conjunction with hospital interns or similar positions."

Upper Franconia had a quota of two Jewish attendants: Dr. Leo Steinberger, Bayreuth, and Dr. Siegmund Bauchwitz, Bamberg. All other Jewish physicians in the district were summarily barred from the profession. Their only task was to give a helping hand in their own liquidation: "Jewish physicians prohibited to practice, as of Sept. 30, 1938, must remove their shingles. I ask you to follow up every case and, if necessary, to enforce the regulation." This, from a letter sent by the district office of the Medical Association of Upper Franconia (dated Oct. 7, 1938, in the Year 6 [presumably the sixth year of the Nazi regime]) to the steward of the Union of Physicians in the German National Health Insurance System in Bamberg. This person devoted himself to the task with the esprit de corps of a true physician. On October 10, he reported to Bayreuth: "A check at all locations of former Jewish physicians assured me that all signs have been removed."

In the middle of the year 1940, the governing body of the medical profession discussed this curious situation: Due to "labor conscription" (read: forced labor) Jewish workers were, according to the law, covered by the National Health System. The question arose: Shall Jewish patients covered by the system be treated by the Jewish medical attendants, or were they required to visit the German doctor assigned by the system? The latter was not in accordance with the rules of the visionaries of racial purity. This was a real dilemma. Dr. Bauchwitz applied for permission to practice in the framework of the national system. Here is his letter:

To the agent for Jewish medical attendants
Dr. Mann
Fürth/Bavaria

I petition you for a permit to act as medical attendant to the Jewish members of the National Health System, as has been granted to Jewish medical attendants in Nuremberg and Fürth. At this moment, there are 150 members covered by the system and a like number of family dependents in Bamberg and the surrounding district. Due to the expansion of labor conscription, the number of members is growing steadily. The Jewish members of the Health System are very anxious to be treated by a Jewish medical attendant.

Very truly yours,
[signed] Dr. Siegmund Israel Bauchwitz
I am Jewish, I.D. No. A 00022
Issued in Bamberg

The tremendous pressure under which Dr. Bauchwitz had to function can be well imagined. He was the chairman of the executive board of the Jewish community and at the same time was the Jewish medical attendant for the western part of Upper Franconia. He had to deal with the problems of the community and with the "authorities," and added to this was the full-time job of a doctor covering an area from Forchheim in the south to Krinach in the north. He had a difficult task for a general practitioner, forced to treat critical cases that should have been under the care of a specialist.

The pressure caused by this problem led to the following letter (dated July 31, 1941), on the stationery of the Jewish Community of Bamberg, addressed to the branch office of the Union of Physicians of the German Health System, Upper Franconia, in Bayreuth:

I turn to you in the capacity of chairman of the Jewish Community in Bamberg and of medical attendant to plead the case for adequate medical care for Jews in Upper Franconia.

I ask you, please, to give permission to specialists in Upper Franconia to accept patients whom I am unable to treat.

The majority of patients in Bamberg and the surrounding district are in the *Arbeitsdienst* [labor battalions] and consequently mandatory members of the National Health System. It is in the interest of all to restore the patients to their full capacity as workers as soon as possible. Furthermore, I ask you, please, to grant permission to physicians outside Bamberg to attend to bedridden Jewish patients. Considering the great distances involved, I find it impossible to treat all those patients.

The above-mentioned reasons should be valid grounds to justify my requests.

Awaiting your valued reply, I remain yours truly,
Dr. Siegmund Israel Bauchwitz

This letter was referred to the administration of the Reich Medical Association of Bavaria.

Enclosed you will find a letter from the Jewish medical attendant in Bamberg, dated July 31, 1941. We wish to hear your opinion in the light of the anticipated refusal by these specialists, based on the interpretation of the published regulations. Are Jewish specialists available in Fürth or Nuremberg?

In our opinion, by following these regulations, we defeat our own purposes, by preventing the insured Jews from returning to work over a more or less extended period of time.

The "valued" reply is worth a closer scrutiny:

To the Jewish Medical Attendant
Siegmund Bauchwitz, Bamberg
Dr. H/F 8.11.41.

Re: Your letter of 7.31.41.

In all localities where no Jewish medical attendant–specialists are available, German specialists may treat Jews, but only if the latter are unable to visit specialists in Fürth and

Nuremberg or due to heavy workload cannot be spared from their places of employment.

sign. Dr. H.[Hessel], Director

The obtuse wording of the letter leaves one guessing as to its real meaning; but what stands out is the fact that a former esteemed colleague is not addressed as "Mr." or "Dr.med." but as the "Jewish Medical Attendant Siegmund Bauchwitz."

To round out the picture of the kind of medical treatment meted out to Jews, we quote the following notice, classified secret and personal, from the Reich Medical Association to its Bavarian branch (dated Mar. 31, 1942) for distribution to the district chiefs, marked "Personal":

> Re: Food rations for sick Jews
>
> Due to the prevailing state of the food supply, it is impossible to extend supplementary food rations, allocated in case of sickness, to Jews or persons classified as Jews, living in Germany.
>
> It is the responsibility of the manager of the hospital kitchen to enforce the rule under strict confidence and with the utmost secrecy.
>
> Due to the shortage of insulin, Jews are not to be given insulin injections.
>
> I ask you to request from the respective departments a list of Jews diagnosed as diabetics, listing their first and family names, date of birth, and place of residence, and to submit this list to the appropriate local office of the Security Service of the SS. These Jewish persons are to be transferred to the East as soon as possible. It is sufficient to hand in the list of names, etc., with the notation "Diabetic Jews."
>
> I request affirmation of compliance with the above order concerning notification of the Security Service about Jews diagnosed as diabetics.
>
> Heil Hitler!
> sign. Dr. Harrfeld

To top off his troubles as Jewish medical attendant, Dr. Bauchwitz had to deal with the problems of persecution through annoyance and chicanery inherent to the office of chairman of the Jewish Community during those days. The first bulletin of the new executive board (quoted below) gives a foretaste of things to come. Here we have the old well-known problem: Jews are still too conspicuous, their mere existence too much for many Bambergers to take. Evidently, the authorities notified the chairman through official channels. Here is the partial text of the bulletin:

Re: Shopping.

1. Certain incidents compel us to repeat our urgent request, especially addressed to the housewives of our community, to adhere to the following rules: show extreme discretion while shopping, especially when forming queues; do not push or attract attention in any other way (e.g., by ordering large quantities which would obviously exceed the normal needs of a household, loud conversations with other Jewish women, etc.). We are well aware of the needs of worried housewives; but today's situation, with its palpable tension in the air, requires from each and every one of us certain considerations, even personal sacrifices, in the interest of all of us and thereby also in your own interest. . . .

4. Again, we strongly and repeatedly appeal to the intelligence and sense of responsibility of all the women of our community to support us willingly in the attempt to maintain discipline and to avoid any cause for friction.

The transgressions cited above would once have been considered mere trifles, not worth mentioning in the real world. But here they show us the pressure a Jewish woman was subjected to by merely entering a shop constantly aware that by her mere existence she caused provocation. Not only was there no occasion for special privileges, but one had to wait one's turn, and for Jewish women that was after all the Aryan customers were served.

But even "in today's situation, with its palpable tension" (what a choice of words!), there was still room for illusions. An example is the escape into the world of ritual sophistry as shown in the bulletin issued by the rabbinical conference held in the spring of 1940. Entitled *Instructions for Passover 5700/1940*, it was prepared by Chief Rabbi Dr. Carlebach, Hamburg; Rabbi Dr Singermann, Berlin; Rabbi Dr. Grünberg, Berlin; Rabbi Dr. Neuhaus, Frankfurt/Main; and Rabbi Dr. Stein, Cologne.

Instructions
for Passover 5700/1940

Matzos left over from last year (if not infested by mites) may be used.

Meat and sausages permitted during the year, acquired as a gift from abroad, can readily be used.

Cheese, if obtained from the Jewish rationing center (Edam cheese) or received as a gift from abroad, may be used.

Margarine, of permitted brands, can be used, as long as it was put into water before restrictions on *chometz* [food proscribed on Passover] went into effect, i.e., the day before Passover Eve.

Oil can be used without hesitation.

Butter must be immersed in water, preferably in a large container, for at least one hour, if possible before Passover, before it can be eaten.

Coffee unadulterated, whether in the form of roasted or unroasted beans (but only if received as a gift from abroad), as well as pure tea, German tea, or herb tea, sold in the original packages, may be used, as long as it was inspected for infestations, before Passover, by spreading it on a colored sheet of paper.

Coffee substitutes are prohibited.

Cocoa, as long as it was acquired as a gift from abroad.

Cocoa mixtures should not be used under any circumstances.

Cocoa shells, on the other hand, may be used freely.

Sugar, salt, and potato starch should preferably be bought in their original packages. Where this is not possible, make sure the scoop being used to weigh the purchase is absolutely clean.

Raisins, sultanas (seedless raisins), and dried fruit, clean thoroughly before the holidays.

Canned fruit and vegetables (apple sauce, apple slices, carrots, spinach, asparagus, cabbage, celery, mushrooms, and tomato paste) can be used on Passover if they were permissible during the year.

Marmalade. It is advisable to make your own, because the brands on the market are prohibited.

Artificial honey, only if bought from Jewish producers.

Pure honey can be used.

Concentrates from cherries, lemons, raspberries, and strawberries are allowed, if prepared without sugar; but drinks made from fresh fruit, such as lemons, are preferable.

The above-mentioned concentrates should not be used for the four cups during the seder [Passover meal].

Vinegar. Buy vinegar made from minerals. Vinegar containing alcohol is pure *chometz* and strictly prohibited. A good substitute is lemon concentrate.

Milk. It is advisable to obtain milk during the actual milking. Otherwise, the milk must be carefully strained and should only be given to children, the sick, and the infirm. If available, use canned milk.

Because of an acute shortage of victuals, this year we allow the use of legumes, such as peas, beans, and lentils (as far as available). They must be inspected and added to boiling water before cooking.

Rice may be fed to children and the sick, but must be cooked in a separate pot which will then be usable for *chometz* only.

Fresh fruit and vegetables must be washed thoroughly before use.

Herring, wash and skin; smoked fish, remove the skin; canned fish is permissible on Passover.

Ground spices and spice substitutes, such as German spices, etc., which are sold in their original packages, may be used.

Cleaners, cleaning powders such as Ika, IMI, and ATA are permitted.

Egg substitutes, egg powder, etc., cannot be used on Passover. They contain pure *chometz*.

Saccharine (crystals in powder form) may be used.

Dextrose (grape sugar), only in an emergency, for children and the sick.

As a mouthwash use hydrogen peroxide or a solution of aluminum acetate.

The instructions in this bulletin are special modifications for the current year only. In all respects the Passover *dinim* [religious obligations] for future years will remain the same as they always were. Only *yomtovdige* [conforming to the special dietary laws of Passover] kitchenware should be used. The above-mentioned dispensations have no effect on the rules concerning *yomtovdige* utensils.

All are enjoined that the above dispensations can only be justified by the exigencies of the times and shall be null and void in the future. Because we are unable to follow scrupulously and with utmost care the *minhagim* [traditional customs] as we were able to do in previous times, we are doubly obliged to observe as much as we can. To do so with strength and love, so as not to take away from the dignity and sanctity of the Passover laws.

> sign. Chief Rabbi Dr. Carlebach, Hamburg
> sign. Rabbi Dr. Singermann, Berlin
> sign. Rabbi Grünberg, Berlin
> sign. Rabbi Dr. Neuhaus, Frankfurt/Main
> sign. Rabbi Dr. Stein, Cologne

But in stark contrast, reality intrudes! Just let us look at the above-mentioned bulletin, which admonished the Jewish housewives of Bamberg—virtually threatened them—to avoid any semblance of provocation while shopping: by yielding their places in queue; by abstaining from frequent opportunities to make additional purchases; by voluntarily scheduling their shopping hours by mutual agreement, up to the point of foregoing needed purchases at certain times and certain places, just to avoid attracting attention in locations that had to be visited. All this to forestall new measures by the authorities, certainly much more unpleasant; all this for the good of all housewives and their families.

What would have happened if a Jewish housewife, shopping for Passover 1940, had insisted on having the milk directly milked into the pot she had brought along? Here is vox populi on the question of milk supply to the Jews, as quoted in *News of the Reich*, February 16, 1942: ". . . wide circles of the population are irritated by the fact that Jewish children are receiving the same ration of whole milk as German children." And finally, here is a confidential information bulletin from the administration of the NSDAP *Gauleitung* (Nazi Party district headquarters) in Bayreuth (dated October 7, 1942) that clearly reflects the style and character of those in charge:

NSDAP District Headquarters, Bayreuth

Ha. Bayreuth, October 7, 1942

District Administration
Confidential Information No. 22/42
Re: Food rations for Jews

October 19, new regulations for the provision of food to Jews will be instituted in conjunction with the general increase of bread and meat rations for the German population. The essential points concerning the supply of food to Jews are as follows:

1. Jews will not be supplied with meat, eggs, wheat products, whole milk, skim milk, and any other foods distributed locally or under special rationing (especially fruit, vegetables, and fish). They will not receive the supplementary rations of bread and fat allocated to German children and adolescents.

2. They will retain the potato, cabbage, and turnip rations. Jewish children under 6 years of age are entitled to half a liter of skim milk a day.

3. Jewish workers employed for extended hours and on the

night shift or doing manual and heavy work will receive the supplements of this category of workers, but not the basic rations (i.e., the meat supplement, but not the normal ration).

4. Additional shopping hours for the sick, expectant mothers, and nursing mothers are in the future withheld from the Jews nationwide.

5. Food distribution centers are ordered to institute special hours for Jews.

6. Food packages from abroad addressed to Jews will be deducted from their rations. Restricted food, such as pure coffee or tea, will be routed to field hospitals or like institutions. The office of the state police and the customs service are responsible for the execution of the above order.

7. Persons of mixed race with special privileges and, by special request, veterans of the World War who can prove injuries sustained in action are exempted from these regulations. The contents of this propaganda advisory are to be explained to the local branches of the NSDAP [Nazi Party] verbally. Any mention in the press or on the radio is undesirable.

5

Rumors and Premonitions

WHAT WAS LEFT OF COMMUNAL LIFE in those years took place at Zinkenwörth 17, the former White Dove restaurant. After the fire and demolition of the synagogue at Herzog-Max Street the Jewish community was left homeless, and eventually all its activities were concentrated at that address. In the late 1930s, after restaurants in the city and the surrounding district denied service to Jews, the White Dove became the only alternative, a place where one could meet and converse with one's friends. Later on, however, it became the center of the community—housing its administrative office, school, prayer room, social hall, and old-age home—and finally the assembly point for deportations.

The White Dove was now the last refuge for Jewish life in Bamberg. Here one was among one's own people, without fear of abuse or public disrespect. The significance of this institution is clearly shown in the bulletin of June 24, 1940, which also points to the difficulties the community had in keeping the restaurant open.

Re: White Dove

> In order to keep the restaurant in operation, a matter of the utmost interest to all the members of the community, it is absolutely necessary to increase patronage. This is the only

means to cover, to a certain extent, the considerable expenses. It is everyone's duty, regardless of any personal views on this matter, to help us maintain a place of undisturbed tranquility and restfulness.

We ask the members of our community and their guests to visit more frequently and consume more of the meals and beverages offered. (A longer stay will surely enhance this possibility.) We hope this appeal will meet with your understanding and consideration.

The reasons for the reluctance of the community members can only be surmised. On one hand, the financial situation was very bad; assets had shrunk or were in inaccessible accounts and the wages of Jewish employees were extremely low; on the other hand, the above-cited bulletin points to the inhibitions shown by certain individuals (as expressed in the phrase "personal views").

In spite of this dark period, attempts were made to present diversions, such as light entertainment in the style of a cabaret, as shown in this notice (dated March 19, 1941):

> On Sunday, March 23, 1941, at 2:30 p.m., a coffee hour for the benefit of the Jewish Winter Relief will take place in the Mondschein Hall at the White Dove. Entertainment by the WD [White Dove] Mundfunk [see below]. All the members of our community are cordially invited.

Here, irony and deeper meanings are at work. Since the fall of 1939, Jews had been prohibited from using or owning radio sets. Furthermore, since the spring of 1941, they had not been allowed to buy newspapers. The word *Rundfunk* ("wireless broadcast") was turned into *Mundfunk* (an invented word, meaning "broadcast by word of mouth"), thereby transforming something forbidden on the outside into something tolerated in the confines of the White Dove. The term *Mundfunk* was also used as a synonym for "rumors."

Besides the announcement of the coffee hour and a notice of where to order food and food substitutes for Passover in exchange for ration coupons, the bulletin (dated March 16, 1941) contained a hint at the reality facing Jews in the spring of 1941.

> We are compelled to make the following statement: Recently renewed rumors are circulating which have caused apprehension in our community. Again, we emphasize that there is no substance to these rumors. We call on the members of our community to maintain strict discipline and not allow irresponsible rumormongers to cause unnecessary anxiety.

Attempting to quell the circulation of budding rumors by issuing announcements of this kind must have been an exercise in futility. Rumors do not originate in thin air. They are a form of reality created by a populace without information or ill-informed at best. Rumors flourish in times of war and oppression, and grow as they circulate; they expand with repetition: *Fama crescit eundo.*[1] It is a wasted effort to counter rumors with rational arguments or to allay them with simplistic pronouncements (e.g., "We emphasize that there is no substance to these rumors").

We may surmise that the rumors pertained to the constant flow of news about deportations, perhaps to the East, which periodically fed the anxiety of Bamberg's Jews. Beginning in October 1939, shortly after the end of the Polish campaign, two transports left Vienna for Poland, ostensibly for "colonization," i.e., reconstruction in which the Jews were forced to help. A letter from the Jewish community in Vienna to the victims of these relocations advised bringing along construction tools, such as axes, saws, planes, hammers, nails, etc. The facts were different. Some of the deportees were interned in an ill-

---

1 "Rumor grows as it goes" (Ed.).

equipped camp near Nisko. As for those not fit for work, they were deprived of their baggage by the SS and then driven across the border into Soviet-occupied Poland.

The *Generalgouvernement* (the German governmental admin-istration in the conquered territories in the East) was caught unawares by these transports and objected vehemently. This caused a cessation of the "relocation action," albeit only for a short time. In Stettin and Pomerania the war economy was a pretext for declaring an allegedly urgent need for housing. This was the occasion for the first mass deportations in the so-called *Altreich* (prewar Germany). On February 12, 1940, the Jewish population of Stettin was deported to Poland, to an area in the vicinity of Lublin. This action was too big to be concealed and soon caught the attention of the neutral press. The [Swiss] *Neue Zürcher Zeitung* reported that "the deportations took place at night, with very short advance notice, preventing the victims from packing even the barest necessities. They were loaded into freight cars without provisions." On February 15, the Reichs-minister for Information and Propaganda reacted as follows: "The foreign press claims that 1,000 Jews were transported to the *Generalgouvernement*. This report is true, but must be treated with the greatest confidence."

This *Nacht und Nebel* action, in the truest sense of the words, caused some discomfort in government circles.[2] The reports in the foreign press triggered troublesome inquiries at the Foreign Ministry, which advised the "chief of police" of the bad impres-sion created abroad, especially in the United States, and urged, in the light of current foreign policy, that the deportations must cease. Through the intervention of Goering in his capacity as chairman of the Ministerial Council of Defense, the deporta-

---

2 The alliterated phrase *Nacht und Nebel*, meaning "under the cover of darkness" (lit. "night and fog"), was widely used in post–World War I Germany.

tions stopped on March 24, 1940, but not before an additional trainload of Jews from Pomerania was dispatched to Lublin.

The ruling circles of the Third Reich were very well aware of all that occurred in the first months of 1940. This can be deduced from an anonymous letter addressed to the chief of the Reich Chancellery, Reichsminister Lammers, who then forwarded it to Heinrich Himmler. The letter describes the fate of the people from Stettin who were pulled from their residences during the night of February 12 and shipped to Poland.

> Men, women, and children were forced to march from Lublin to their final destination along a road covered with deep snow at a temperature of -20 degrees Celsius [-4 degrees Fahrenheit]. This was a march of untold heart-rending scenes. Of the 1,200 who left Stettin, 72 succumbed during the 14-hour march, among them men and women up to the age of 86. Most of the victims froze to death. A mother was cradling her 3-year-old child in her arms, trying to protect it from the bitter cold with her own garments. Succumbing to the barbaric hardship she fell by the wayside, still holding her child, which was found nearly frozen to death. Around her neck was a cardboard reading "Renate Alexander of Hammerstein, Pomerania." The child was visiting relatives in Stettin and was deported with them, while her parents remained in Germany. Her hands and feet had to be amputated in a Lublin hospital. After the transport passed the corpses were picked up along the highway by sled and buried in the cemeteries of Piaski and Lublin.

Undoubtedly, knowledge about these events, even without all the gory details, reached beyond the inner circle of those involved to the neutral press, as can be seen by the reportage. Half-truths circulated in the form of rumors among the general population. The rumors were repressed by non-Jews, while those somehow affected regarded them as an omen of their own future and passed them on.

One event alarmed German Jewry more than any other, because it was a relatively new development. On November 22, 1940, 7,000 Jews in Baden and the Saar/Palatinate were rounded up by auxiliary police and deported to unoccupied France with very little baggage for a long journey. This was a private raid by the two district leaders, Rudolf Wagner and Joseph Bürckel, who claimed to have acted on the authority of a Führer Order. They were just a little ahead of schedule. Official documents touching on these events (e.g., one issued by the Reich Foreign Ministry) tie the deportations to France to a plan for the resettlement of 270,000 German and East European Jews in Madagascar.

The Vichy government was outraged by this imposition. It housed close to 7,000 Jews in ill-kept barracks in the foothills of the Pyrenees. Postal service between France and the neutral countries was still available, and the living conditions in the camps soon became widely known.

Eventually, something unheard of occurred. A German newspaper, the *Badische Presse* of February 14, 1941, reported on the life of the deported Jews in France; this was to remain the only instance of a semiofficial report on the fate of deported Jews in the German press.

> Leben wie Gott in Frankreich
>   of the Fugitive Traitors!
> Life in the Gurs Emigration Camp!

> . . . Conditions in this camp are so severe, according to one account, that those who have not seen or experienced it would not believe it possible. In the camp at Vernet, once-strong men, now weakened by hunger and cold, have lost all resemblance to human beings.

. . . In the concentration camp at Gurs, an average of 45 people die every week. We lie on the bare floor without mattresses or straw and with only two thin blankets while the temperature drops to -10 Celsius [14° Fahrenheit].

. . . A quick calculation based on the average number of deaths (without anticipating any kind of epidemic) will show that half of the camp population will have died within two years.

Disregarding the accusations which called the deported Jews of Baden and the Palatinate "fugitive traitors," this reportage is without parallel in the entire press of the Third Reich. Never again was there an exposé of life in a camp (even of those in unoccupied France) as depicted here.

The article's author and editor must have realized almost immediately that they had done a disservice to all the agencies involved in the Jewish Question. There was no reprint in any other German newspaper. The true picture was too stark.

Presumably some details of the report filtered into regions beyond the *Badische Presse*'s circulation area and were the basis of widespread rumors about the fate of German Jewry in days to come. In due time the rumors reached Bamberg. Dr. Bauchwitz's efforts to calm the members of his community, and to convince them that the rumors were just that and no more, were in all likelihood fruitless.

In the meantime, the decrees in no way ceased appearing. On January 23, 1940, a directive of the Reich Ministry of Economic Affairs halted the distribution of clothing ration cards to Jews. "There will be absolutely no cards issued to Jews for cloth garments, shoes, and shoe leather. Jews will be supplied by the Reichsvereinigung specifically with second-hand merchandise available without cards." In this light we may understand the establishment of the storeroom for clothing, mentioned above, which collected used clothing and distributed it to the needy.

There was always a shortage; after all, a community whose members' lives were very restricted was not the most fertile ground for generous donations. An edict of the chief of Party Headquarters, dated June 26, 1941, seems almost absurd today. It prohibited the distribution of shaving soap to Jews. The cruelty is obvious; in the perception of those days, unshaven Jews looked so much more "Jewish." The intent becomes clear; without ration cards for clothing and soap a decrepit underclass develops—one with a shabby appearance, ready to be classified as asocial and become the target for abuse. The goal of this propaganda was to push the Jew into the criminal underworld as a depraved individual.

In the summer and fall of 1941, the trickle of laws and regulations turned into a flood. On September 5, the infamous Police Ordinance On the Identification of Jews was published, and on September 14, a bulletin of the Jewish community notified the members:

District Office of the Reichvereinigung
Bavaria
Bamberg Branch Office

Bamberg, September 14, 1941

To all our members:
Re: Police Ordinance on the Identification of Jews
  (RGB1 I. No. 100 of Sept. 5, 1941 S.547)

Enclosed you will find a copy of the Police Ordinance on the Identification of Jews as of September 1, 1941. The instructions for implementation of the ordinance are as follows:
The ordinance takes effect on Friday the 19th of this month.

In Bamberg identification badges will be issued on Thursday, September 18, in our office, at the following hours:
10:00 a.m.–12 noon for members with the letters A–K
3:00 p.m.–6:00 p.m. for members with the letters L–Z
6:00 p.m.–7:00 p.m. for employed men and women.

No one is allowed to pick up badges for another person, with the exception of spouses.

The badges can only be issued against a personal signature.

Persons employed in Bamberg but residing elsewhere receive their badges at their place of residence.

There will be absolutely no exemptions to the identification law, and therefore refrain from submitting petitions.

From the day the decree becomes effective, in this case Friday, the 19th of this month, Jews are prohibited from appearing in public without badges. Without diminishing the penalties contained in the order, failure to comply with these rules can be counted on to bring additional measures from the authorities.

With the introduction of identification badges we expect every Jew to adhere to the prescribed obligations and to show even greater restraint in public. Every Jew must now be more aware than ever that, through his actions and his conduct in public, he is responsible for the welfare of our entire community.

Very respectfully yours,
Dr. Siegmund Isr. Bauchwitz

The Reich Ministry of Transportation did not want to be left out. From September 18 on, Jews were prohibited from using public transportation and from leaving their town of residence. They were not allowed to use vehicles of any kind, except for bicycles needed to reach the place of forced labor assignment. The community office had on hand the appropriate printed forms to be submitted to the labor exchange for an exemption.

Certification

The Jew _____ born on _____

residing at _____

employed by _____

for labor assignment.

This is to certify that due to lack of other means of transportation, applicant must use a bicycle to reach his place of
employment.

City _____, on _____ 1941

Labor Office

This was pure chicanery, intended to torment and rattle the
victim and slowly change him from a human being to a cog in
the bureaucratic machine. To top it off, a regulation was published in the *Jüdisches Nachrichtenblatt* in Berlin on February 12,
1942 prohibiting Jews from keeping house pets.

But more than mere chicanery was a decree issued by Reich
Security Service Headquarters (RSHA), Section IV B 4, dated
October 23, 1941, "banning the emigration of Jews, without
exception, for the duration of the war."

Section IV B 4 of RSHA was the office of Adolf Eichmann.
The first in Bamberg to feel the grave consequences of this
decree were Max and Lina Ehrlich, who, despite the ever-wors-
ening world political situation, actively pursued their emigration to the United States. On October 23, 1941, the lord mayor
of Bamberg made a routine inquiry of the Gestapo in Nuremberg asking if there were any objections to the emigration of the
Ehrlichs. The answer was short and unequivocal.

Secret State Police
Nuremberg/Fürth Office

Nuremberg 1, P.O. Box 210
Telephone No. 2951
P.O. Account Nuremberg No. 35695
No. 7280/41 II B 4

Nuremberg, Nov. 1, 1941

To the Lord Mayor of the City of Bamberg
Re: Emigration of Jews, in this case, Ehrlich Couple
Subject: Your letter of Oct. 23, 1941
Enclosures: ./.

According to orders from the Reichsführer-SS and the Chief of the German Police Forces, all emigration of Jews must be stopped, effective immediately.

     as per
     (sign.)

6

The End: Deportations

AN OMINOUS TURN in regard to the Jewish Question was now affirmed. Expulsion to foreign countries or the creation of a Jewish state, whether in the area of Lublin or on the island of Madagascar, was no longer the goal. Now the aim was complete physical annihilation. Available sources leave no doubt that Hitler himself was the guiding spirit. Coded language by those involved could hardly conceal the grim facts; only apologists, denying the existence of a Nazi race doctrine, can doubt the real meaning behind the words.

On October 14 and 21, 1941, Kurt Daluege, chief of the security police, signed two orders for the expulsion of a total of 50,000 Jews from the Altreich, the Ostmark, and the Reichskommissariat Ostland (German-occupied territory in the East). The transports, consisting of about 1,000 people each, were to be handled by the German National Railroad. This triggered a voluminous correspondence between Section IV B 4 of the RHSA (Security Service Headquarters) and the National Railroad.

Regrettably, source material for Bamberg is scarce; but contemporaneous documents from other cities reveal a vivid picture of the events that must have taken place in Bamberg at this time. The Gestapo in Nuremberg/Fürth was in charge. To be precise, enforcement was in the hands of Sturmbannführer [Lieutenant] Dr. Theodor Grafenberger, who did his job with extreme precision. Presumably, procedures were the same as in other cities: The administration of the Jewish community received orders from the "authorities" to pick a certain number of members to be included in the next transport, the victims to be chosen without regard to age or illness, even including disabled war veterans and those decorated during World War I.

We do not know how or by what criteria Dr. Bauchwitz made the selections; but we can well imagine the excruciatingly painful and hopeless situation in which he was caught. The original list of the first transport of Jews deported from Bamberg did not survive the war, but laborious postwar research in the card files of the Registrar's Office produced the names of the victims. Following guidelines to conceal the real meaning of the deportations to the East, the only notation found on the cards was "Evacuated on 11.27.41."

There was more to the onerous task of selections. The Jewish community's administrative office, as a branch of the Reichsvereinigung der Juden in Deutschland, was forced to notify the victims of their fate and how they were expected to cooperate. In Bamberg none of the notices has surfaced, but notifications from other localities are on hand and give us a clear example of the contents and what the shaken victims, crushed by the worst fears over their fate, were told. This is the text of a letter circulated in Stuttgart on November 19, 1941; a notification in Bamberg would not have varied by much.

Union of Jewish Communities in Wurttemberg

Stuttgart, Nov. 19, 1941
Hospital Street 36
Your transport number:
Please note carefully

Mr./Mrs./Miss
and children:
Enclosures
Re: Evacuation

By order of the Secret State Police, Stuttgart Directorate, we hereby notify you that you and your above-mentioned children have been assigned to an evacuation transport to the East. At the same time we advise you that you and your children assigned to the above-mentioned transport must be ready at your present place of residence, starting Wednesday, Nov. 26, 1941. You are prohibited from leaving the premises, even for a short period of time, without a special permit from the authorities.

Forced labor assignments, even in essential industries, do not give exemption from this evacuation order.

Attempts to resist or evade evacuation are useless and will only lead to grave consequences for those concerned.

The enclosed declarations of assets, filled out carefully and separately for each family member, including children, must be turned in to the local police authorities within three days.

Also enclosed is a list of the most essential articles needed for the trip.

Take note that every evacuee is allowed to bring up to 50 kilograms of baggage, whether in suitcases, knapsacks, or shoulder bags. We recommend that most of the baggage be carried in knapsacks. It must be taken into account that transport participants will have to carry their own baggage for an extended span of time. Suitcases, knapsacks, and blankets must be clearly identified with above transport number. In addition, it is also advisable to add the full name. If possible, use indelible ink and sturdy baggage tags. We recommend wearing warm underwear, warm garments, the most sturdy boots or shoes, overshoes, coats, and caps (rather than hats).

In addition to hand baggage, it is permissible to take along mattresses, some linen, some kitchen utensils (but not kitchen furniture), groceries, canned food, first aid kits, sewing kits, nails, and house and garden tools. It is anticipated that a few stoves with exhaust pipes and sewing machines (preferably the self-contained sort) will be permitted to be taken along. Of utmost importance are spades, shovels, and other construction tools.

The above-mentioned articles should be kept separate in your apartment and packed together, if possible. Sharp tools must be wrapped securely. These articles, especially mattresses, must carry the transport number on durable identification tags; they must be listed on the declaration forms with the comment "to accompany the transport."

From the time you receive this letter, you are not allowed access to your assets, as per strict orders of the authorities. You can no longer sell, give away, lend, charge against, or make any other use of your assets.

Every transport participant will receive a voucher in the amount of 50 reichmarks from the Reich Credit Bank and two packages for the price of 7.65 reichmarks, one containing food for the trip, the other flour, legumes, etc., to be transported as baggage.

The amount of 57.65 reichmarks for each person must be submitted immediately, either to the office of the Union of Jewish Communities in Württemberg, Stuttgart, Hospital Street 36, or to special account "W" of the Reichsvereinigung der Juden in Deutschland, Württemberg branch at the Gymnasium Street office of the Deutsche Bank, Stuttgart.

In case you are not able to pay the required amount, notify the office of the Union of Jewish Communities immediately. Despite the ban on access to your assets now in force, you can still withdraw your full November allotment, provided you have the required permit.

Before departure, you must turn in your food ration cards with redemption dates of December 1 or later at the appropriate office of the Economic Planning Board, in return for the official certificate of departure. This certificate will enable you to receive the above-mentioned food packages in Stuttgart.

Finally, we ask you not to despair. The achievements of our members at their diverse work assignments justify the hope that they will also master these new and difficult tasks.

> Union of Jewish Communities in Württemberg
> Ernst Israel Moos
> Theodor Israel Rothschild
> Alfred Israel Fackenheim

Only two bulletins concerning impending deportations in Bamberg have been found, dated November 21 and 22, 1941.

> Reichsvereinigung der Juden in Deutschland
> Bavaria District Office
> Bamberg Branch

> Bamberg, Nov. 22, 1941

> By order of the authorities, all members of the community must remain at their places of residence on Saturday, until noon.
> sign. Dr. Siegmund Israel Bauchwitz

The sparse wording attracts attention and portends the worst. Dr. Bauchwitz's way with words, able to convey bad tidings in an acceptable style, deserted him. What remains is a sobering statement: that they have been asked to remain at home "by order of the authorities." Saturday, November 22, was evidently the day the ominous letters were delivered, letters that put an end to the way of life known until then.

The bulletin of November 22 clearly shows the difficulties encountered by the community and all those on the deportation list.

Reichsvereinigung der Juden in Deutschland
Bavaria District Office
Bamberg Branch

Bamberg, Nov. 22, 1941

To the members of our community!

1. Not a single delivery of warm woolen garments and good
   footwear has reached us. We must now turn to those not
   on the list of deportees and ask them to bring to the community office, all day Sunday, woolen articles (underwear
   and outer garments for men as well as women) and footwear that are in good condition. This is the least we can do
   for our departing brothers and sisters. We expect everyone
   to fulfill his obligation to the best of his ability.
   The following items are also urgently needed: suitcases,
   knapsacks, woolen blankets, woolen scarfs, sashes, ear-
   muffs, mittens, first aid articles, and medicines.

2. Distribution of woolen clothing for deportees is scheduled
   for Monday, starting at 9:00 a.m.

3. Employees of the Municipal Department of Public Works
   who are on the deportation list must pick up their pay and
   papers at the gasworks at the department offices.

4. Those not scheduled for deportation must report to work
   at the regular time Monday morning.

5. Those who would like to have their ghetto baggage
   weighed can report to the community office on Sunday.

6. Those unable to carry their own knapsacks to the Dove on
   evacuation day must notify us on Sunday.

sign. Dr. Siegmund Israel Bauchwitz
sign. Helene Sara Eckstein

The shortage of winter clothing is easily understood. With
the cancellation of clothing ration cards, Jews were unable to
replace their worn garments. Photos of Jews ready for transport

clearly illustrate the shabby appearance of the formerly well-appointed bourgeoisie. The bulletin of November 22 shows that the community administration was no longer sure whether the reports of terrible conditions during resettlements were mere rumors. The terminology "ghetto baggage" smacks of old hatreds and leaves a bad aftertaste. Wasn't it the firm belief of Bavarian Jewry that they had escaped from the ghetto in 1813? The choice of the word "ghetto" must have led to the image of restricted housing in circumscribed space under distress and threat. We do not know what answers were given to the questions the deportees most certainly would have asked the communal administration: "Where are we going? What will we find there?" We cannot know what sort of solace was offered. But one thing is certain: The onus was on the people running the Jewish community. They were the ones who had to do the explaining and the comforting.

Procedures in small towns were different, since their Jewish communities were not self-governing bodies and thus there were no Jewish community boards to preside over the liquidation. Deportation lists were compiled by the local police. They handled this with the bureaucracy's typically officious eagerness and petit-bourgeois attitude. Citizens of irreproachable character were treated like vagrants or petty thieves, the same legalistic language being used to arrest them and escort them out of town. The meticulous code of the German civil service manifested itself at its most perverted!

Documents concerning the first major deportations in Franconia were found in the files of the county seat in Forchheim.

Forchheim, Nov. 22, 1941

To the Mayor of the City of Forchheim
Re: List of Jews to be evacuated from Forchheim/Upper Franconia

As per notification from Criminal Inspector Bezold, Bamberg, a list of Jews to be evacuated from Forchheim must be submitted to the Nuremberg/Fürth state police office, attention Commissioner Woesch. It must arrive there on Nov. 22, 1941. Enclosed is the provisional list.

Secretary of the Criminal Police

The "provisional list" in its entirety is reproduced in Table 2.

TABLE 2. Jews to be evacuated from Forchheim, Upper Franconia

Name	Occupation	Date of Birth	Birthplace	Address
Abraham, Leo Jarnel	Merchant	Jan. 8, 1875	Hohnhausen V.B. Brake	Forchheim, Paradeplatz 4
Abraham, geb. Gröschel, Jenny Sara	Housewife	Feb. 8, 1877	Forchheim	Forchheim, Paradeplatz 4
Braun, Gottlieb Israel	Merchant, now assistant	Apr. 26, 1875	Kunreuth near Forchheim	Forchheim, Paradeplatz 4
Braun, geb. Asch, Rosa Sara	Housewife	May 9, 1883	Wilhelmsdorf Merktlerbach	Forchheim, Paradeplatz 4
Israel, geb. Braun, Ilse Sara	Housewife	Sep. 28, 1911	Forchheim	Forchheim, Paradeplatz 4
Heller, Flora Sara	None	Mar. 13, 1886	Forchheim	Forchheim, Wiesentstrasse 16
Schönberger, Ida Sara	None	Mar. 11, 1885	Krareuth near Forchheim	Forchheim, Paradeplatz 4
Zeidler, Grete Sara	None	Nov. 30, 18.89	Schaussberg near Berlin	Forchheim, Wiesentstrasse 16
Reserve:				
Sundheimer, Berta Sar[a]	None	Nov. 10, 1872	Mittlereilersbach	Forchheim, Wiesentstrasse 1
Tiesler, Rosa Sara	Widow	May 30, 1875	Zempelburg near Flatow	Forchheim, Hornschuhallee 4

The verbose pomposity of the secretary of the criminal police in Forchheim in his final report to the mayor of Forchheim discloses some details of the deportation of November 1941; among other things, that the transport left from Nuremberg, using freight cars, routed to Riga.

File No. 168/41

Forchheim, Nov. 27, 1941

Criminal Police
Forchheim, Upper Franconia

To the Mayor of the City of Forchheim
Re: Evacuation of Jews to the East

The following local Jews were transported to the East: Abraham, Leo Israel; Abraham, née Gröschel, Jenny Sara; Braun, Gottlieb Israel; Braun, née Asch, Rosa Sara; Israel, née Braun, Ilse Sara; Heller, Flora Sara; Schönberger, Ida Sara and Zeidler, Grete Sara. They were transported today, at 9:00 a.m., by truck to Bamberg. From there, they will travel by rail to Nuremberg, to leave on Nov. 29, 1941 by freight train for Riga. They were escorted by Police Sergeant N— and SS Trooper L—. A considerable number of local residents witnessed the deportation with great interest and expressed their immense satisfaction.

The seven Jews remaining in town are elderly and feeble. We hope to transfer them in the near future to the old-age home in Bamberg.

The apartments of the evacuated Jews were locked and placed under seal. Keys are in the hands of the Forchheim municipal administration.

It is absolutely certain that by Christmas 1941 Forchheim will be free of Jews.

Secretary of the Criminal Police

In reality, the history of the Jews in Forchheim only came to an end on April 24, 1942. At that time the secretary of the criminal police reported to the mayor of Forchheim that Rosa Tiesler, the last Jewish resident of Forchheim, had been "deported by the undersigned to Bamberg."

The deportation list in Bamberg contained 106 names. Presumably, "none of them employed in economically essential enterprises," in accordance with the guidelines of the Reich Finance Ministry, published on November 4, 1941. These are the statistics: 46 males (43.40%), 60 females (56.60%). The average age was 50.8 years. There were 10 youths (under the age of 20): Jacob Ansbacher, 18; Susi Böhm, 12; Carola Freudenthal, 11; Max Gunzenhäuser, 17; Ruth Gunzenhäuser, 13; Walter Gunzenhäuser, 17; Ilse Lipp, 15; Ruth Schapiro, 16; Elisabeth Walter, 16; and Helga Walter, 13. The above group lowered the average age to a certain extent; but still, it was obviously an "old" transport. This gives us an idea of the methods used in the selection: Most of the selectees were close to retirement age, around 65, or the younger members of their families. Here are some examples: Albert Walter (a war veteran with serious war injuries) was 57 and his daughter Helga Walter was 13. Eight members of the Forchheimer family, two men and six women, were all, with one exception, over 50, the average age 55.9.

From the moment the deportation notice arrived, the normal life of the victims came to an end. They were caught in a net of demands and regulations, issued by the authorities, ruling their personal lives and assets. They were forced to implement their own elimination from rightful citizenship by dutifully filling out a heap of worthless forms, by registering their own departure, and by making payments; all this causing an endless round of office visits. The Stuttgart documents show this very clearly, and the situation in Bamberg could not have been much different.

"Evacuations," the code word used in all official documents to hide the real events, were a new challenge for the bureaucracy involved. Never before had anyone tossed out an entire segment of the population. This situation necessitated precautionary steps, leading to a mass of regulations that make the immediate circumstances of the deportations of November 1941 clear to us. The Nuremberg/Fürth state police bureau became the office responsible for the execution of the deportations in Lower, Middle, and Upper Franconia. Deportees from the entire territory of Franconia were to be collected at Nuremberg/Langwasser to start their journey to the Reichskommissariat Ostland [conquered territory in the East]. SS Major Dr. Martin, the chief of the local office of the state police, was in overall charge. Lieutenant Dr. Grafenberger was responsible for the administration. The task was handled with perfect precision, meticulously organized to the smallest detail, as shown in the directive for the procedures to be followed at deportations of Jews issued by Grafenberger on November 19, 1941. As early as November 19, a notification was sent from Nuremberg to the criminal police in Bamberg, advising them that a certain number of Jews would be evacuated by the end of November, and that the transport would have to be abundantly supplied with equipment.

> Basically, the following are to be supplied for every 100 *Ev.-Nr.* ["evacuation numbers," i.e., individuals deported]: 1 iron stove with exhaust pipes, a large boiling kettle, and 1 roll of barbed wire; in addition, per 100 Jews: 2 window panes 25.7 cm x 34.3 cm and 5 window panes 27 cm x 44 cm, 1 shovel, and 1 ax. The Jews themselves are responsible for procurement, since there is no question of the authorities holding preliminary discussions with the respective administrative service in this matter. All above-mentioned materials will be known as ghetto equipment.

The document, further on, makes a revealing statement: "Procurement is less for the benefit of the Jews than for the need to satisfy the offices of the relocation authorities in the East, which will otherwise refuse to accept further transports." The order to bring along construction tools, hand tools, sewing machines, stoves, and similar objects on the transport might lead Jews to infer that the evacuations were a real attempt at colonization of the East. This mistaken belief was quite welcome, and the "authorities" fostered it by additional references in the requisitions. Of course, the "authorities knew better"—even as the relatively advanced average ages of the transportees speaks against any assignment to land reclamation. The term "ghetto equipment" would help create a more tranquil and, to a certain extent, more confident state of mind. At the same time, the equipment provided the relocation authorities in the East with material for building the camps and probably for the black market and barter. It goes without saying that once the deportees arrived in the East they never laid eyes on the equipment, which had often been acquired with the greatest difficulty.

The same week that Jews in Franconia had to accept resettlement in the East, the *Reich Law Gazette* published a decree under the title "Eleventh Amendment to the German Citizenship Law," a text which had far-reaching significance for the future treatment of the so-called Jewish Question. Despite the pseudoscientific prattle about the purity of the Aryan race, the Final Solution to the Jewish Question had a down-to-earth economic aspect. All those involved in actions against Jews tried to enrich themselves to the greatest extent possible; and since the Third Reich was known for strict order, the continuous plunder of the victims had to be given the appearance of law and order, which was created by the Eleventh Amendment to the Citizenship Law.

In accordance with the German Citizenship Law of September 15, 1935, §3 . . . , the following is decreed:
§1
A Jew with permanent residence abroad cannot be a German citizen. Regular residence outside the country by a Jew under these circumstances which becomes known shall be considered as permanent residence abroad.
§2
A Jew relinquishes his German citizenship,
(a) if his permanent residence at the inception of this decree is abroad.
(b) If he later takes up residence abroad with the intention to remain there permanently, from the time that this decree takes effect.
§3
(1) Assets of Jews who relinquish their citizenship in accordance with this decree will, at the moment of loss of citizenship, become the property of the Reich. Furthermore, assets of Jews who become stateless through this decree and who formerly were German citizens, shall become the property of the Reich if they are or become foreign residents.
(2) The surrendered assets shall serve as support for all needs in solving the Jewish Question.
§ 4
(1) Persons who surrender their assets under §3 of the decree cannot become heirs to the property of German citizens.
(2) Gifts by German citizens to persons who surrender their assets to the Reich under §3 of the decree are prohibited. Those who disregard the law and present or promise gifts will be punished with up to two years in prison or a fine or both.
§5
(1) The German Reich is responsible for the debts of Jews who surrender their assets, only up to the amount of the value of forfeited property and rights. There will be no responsibility for debts that run counter to the sentiment of the people of the Reich.

(2) Previous claims against assets surrendered to the German Reich remain valid.

(3) In case of a debit balance, the Reich Minister of Finance or the creditors can use the bankruptcy courts to register their claims against the forfeited assets in accordance with the laws of bankruptcy. The chief of the Finance Department in Berlin will appoint an administrator of bankrupt assets and can summon him as needed.

§6

(1) In case a Jew who surrenders his assets to the Reich under §3 is required by law or by mutual agreement to support a third party, the Reich will not assume responsibility for support payments due after the forfeit of the assets. However, the Reich can compensate non-Jewish claimants, as long as they reside within Germany's borders.

(2) Compensation can be in the form of cash; however, it may not exceed the value of the assets surrendered to the Reich.

(3) Compensation can also be in the form of objects or rights that are part of the forfeited assets. There shall be no fee for the services of the court.

§7

(1) All persons who are in possession of any part of the forfeited assets or are in debt to the assets in bankruptcy must report these facts to the chief of the Finance Department in Berlin immediately at the inception of the Surrender Law (§3). Those who intentionally or unintentionally fail to comply with above regulations will be subject to up to three months imprisonment or a fine.

(2) Claims against forfeited assets must be filed within six months after the inception of the Surrender Law (§3) with the chief of the Finance Department in Berlin. Claims submitted after the above-mentioned deadline can be rejected without cause.

§8

(1) Decisions regarding the requirements for forfeiture under the Law are the responsibility of the chief of the Security Police and the SD [Nazi Party security service].

(2) Administration and utilization of surrendered assets are the responsibility of the chief of the Finance Department in Berlin....

§10

(1) Claims for support of Jews who lose their German citizenship under §2 expire at the end of the month the citizenship was revoked.

(2) If, according to support regulations, dependents are entitled to payments after the death of another claimant, such as support for widows, orphans, supplementary relief, or similar compensation, they will receive payment as long as they reside within Germany's borders at the time of the expiration of support, as per paragraph (1); non-Jewish dependents will receive full support payments up to the sum stipulated in the regulations. Jewish dependents will receive half of the stipulated payments. Supplements for children will be paid only to non-Jewish claimants....

§12

This law is also applicable in the Protectorate ... and in the annexed territories in the East.

The infamy of this law is quite obvious. The territories to which Jews were deported were arbitrarily declared "foreign countries," thereby justifying revocation of German citizenship. Absolutely none of the people placed on the deportation lists at the end of November voluntarily opted for a stay "abroad." The real importance of the declaration of assets among all the formalities the victims had to undergo now becomes clear. Again and again it was emphasized that the forms had to be completed "carefully" and that failure to do so would incur "heavy penalties," even as one asks just which "heavy penalties" can be applied to victims who have to finance their own journey to the place of their execution? If we spare the description of the format of the declaration of assets forms, we can be sure they were just another link in the policy of cooperation in one's own extinction, since the Nazis demanded meticulous adherence to orders by their victims. Everything was covered by the words of the law and the text of the decrees; the ruling authorities were well aware of the impact of their actions. Taking this for granted, it is understandable that an entire army of faithful bureaucrats repressed any pangs of conscience and became willing collaborators in the official crimes.

November 27, 1941, a Thursday, was the day fixed for the deportation of Bamberg's Jews; the assembly point was the White Dove. We may assume that the procedures were not much different from those followed in Würzburg or Frankfurt. After the victims arrived at the White Dove, presumably under police escort—after all, this was an "arrest" followed by "expulsion"—the meager baggage was searched for contraband and finally there was a strip-search for concealed objects of value. In Würzburg a midwife was summoned to take on this task. Then the "carefully completed" declarations of assets were collected, followed immediately by the pronouncement of a bailiff that all these assets were now the property of the Reich.

We can well imagine the contents of the notifications composed by the police and issued by the Jewish community for delivery on November 22 to the Jews of Bamberg: a request to be prepared for "arrest" in the early morning hours of Thursday, November 27, 1941. The scenario is described in detail in a Memorandum to Assigned Officers from the Frankfurt Gestapo.

> I expect that you will execute your assignment with the force, correctness, and precision required. . . .
> You are to proceed as follows:
> 1. At the appointed time, go to the Jewish residence assigned

to you. If the Jews refuse entry and do not open the door, one of you is to remain near the apartment while the other must notify the nearest police precinct immediately.

Inside the Jewish residence assemble all the members of the family and read them the order of the state police (attached to this memorandum).

The Jews are to remain in one room, assigned by you. A second official is to stay with the members of the Jewish family at all times. You will deal with the head of household yourself.

2. Inspect the residence with the head of household. No additional fuel is to be added to lit furnaces. In the case of slow-combustion stoves (tile stoves, etc.), unscrew the furnace door to give the fire a chance to burn down while you are still in the Jewish apartment. When you leave the residence, all fires must be extinguished. . . .

4. Woolen blankets which are part of the baggage allowance must be either rolled up or folded in a way that they can be easily transported.

5. Accompany the head of household through the residence (including cellars and attics) and take note of food supplies and living animals inside the residence. If possible, collect above items, with the help of the head of household, in the [outer] hallway of the residence. Notify the N.S.V. [Nazi Party Relief Organization] and arrange for the removal of these items.

6. The Jew must collect all objects of value, bankbooks, securities, jewelry, and cash above the limits of the allotment. These objects or valuables must be handed to you, registered, and packed in a bag or envelope. Close the receptacle and mark the first and family names, city, and address of the owner on the front. . . .

7. Ask the Jews to show you their identification papers, which later are to be surrendered at the assembly point.

8. All objects which are to be removed (suitcases, house keys) must be marked with durable tags showing the name and

address of the Jewish owner. Tags must be attached in a secure way that will prevent them from getting detached. The writing must be clearly legible. Tags must be prepared at the residence and securely attached to the above-mentioned objects. Furthermore, every Jew must wear a placard around his neck with his name, date of birth, and I.D. number.

9. After inspection of apartment, cellar, and attic, which—I repeat emphatically—must be done in the presence of the Jewish head of household, one of the officers will accompany the Jews to the designated assembly point. . . .

All official papers had to be surrendered, as well as workman's passes and ration cards, with the exception of the I.D. card, which was stamped EVACUATED, as the only remaining proof of a legal existence. This was the straw that broke the camel's back. Now the victims saw clearly the end product of the entire procedure: the destruction, not only of their civil, but also of their physical, existence.

In this manner, 114 persons were "dispatched." This, of course, took some time, because it, too, was done with the usual care. How the transport moved from Zinkenwörth to the freight ramp at the railroad station (behind the customs office) is not known. Did they walk, or were they driven by truck or bus? A Bamberger who was then 14 years old remembers gray buses parked on Schillerplatz, and a member of the guard detail urging him to move on or risk being taken along. Whether this recollection refers to the November deportation is not certain.

During the afternoon of November 27, the Bambergers arrived in Nuremberg/Langwasser, where a collection point for approximately 1,000 deportees to the East was established on the site of the Nazi Party convention grounds. In his bureaucratic and pedantic way, Grafenberger issued the order of the day regulating life at the collection camp. One thing became immediately clear to everyone sent there: their usual bourgeois life had come to an end, even the restricted existence known since 1938. Yet, in retrospect, it would have been considered the height of freedom compared to events to come.

Just what the Nuremberg assembly camp looked like is unknown, since photos and films shot for documentation have disappeared. It could not have differed much from the one in Stuttgart. Pictures taken there show a large room full of mattresses and baggage with people sitting or moving about. Food was provided—charged to the Jewish community, of course—by a field kitchen. The deportees stood in line and waited, with ample time to contemplate the dark future. The "authorities," all the way down to the police sergeant in Forchheim, knew the transport was destined to go to Riga; but the deportees did not have the vaguest idea.

The departure from Nuremberg, scheduled for Saturday, November 29, was orchestrated down to the most minute details by Grafenberger, as can be seen in his order of the day.

> Deportation of the Jews via transport train is scheduled for Nov. 29, 1941, at 3:00 p.m. . . . At 12.45 p.m., the loaded train will become the responsibility of the commander of the transport, First Lieutenant L—. He will also recruit the escort troops.
>
> The schedule for loading on Nov. 29, 1941 is as follows:
>
> At 8:00 a.m., detail trucks arrive in front of each ghetto barrack. They transfer all the accompanying baggage, except for mess kits, to the staging area in front of the evacuation train, to arrive there not later than 9:00 a.m. Jewish personnel will be assigned to do the work. Chalk marks already on the train direct specific evacuation numbers to their assigned cars. The freight handlers must unload the baggage in front of the respective cars, as per designated evacuation numbers. SS escort troops and SS guards will take over from here. The transport personnel cannot be used at this point.

Baggage transfer is supervised by Chief Clerk S—. He will have the support of those in charge of the evacuation. At 9:00 a.m. all able-bodied Jews, with the exception of those on kitchen duty, must line up. They will be marched, under guard, to their assembled baggage. Mess kits, etc., must remain in the ghetto barracks for later meals. At the assembly point Jewish orderlies direct the Jews to pick up their baggage and line up in front of their assigned cars. (They must carry their own hand luggage.) These preliminary arrangements must be completed by 11:00 a.m. The baggage will remain in this location. The Jews will be marched back to the camp for the meal call. By 12:30 p.m., the mess hall must be closed and all barracks must be tidied up. At 12:30 p.m., all Jews must line up in front of the barracks, ready for immediate departure, carrying the mess kits they intend to take along. (All this is the responsibility of the Jewish auxiliaries under the command of the Jew Gustav Kleemann, Würzburg.)

As soon as the Jewish leader reports that the transport is ready, the Jews will march out of the camp to the baggage for the last time. The order to board the train, with luggage in hand, will be given by Chief Clerk F—. At 1:30 p.m., the transport must be ready to move. At 1:45 p.m., the officer in charge of the transport will take command. At 2:00 p.m., the National Railroad will start moving the train out of the freight yard. During this time all SS troops, with the exception of two men guarding the camp, must patrol the rail yards. After the departure of the train, the SS troops will return to the camp. They will receive their pay and be dismissed. The entire operation should be finished by 5:30 p.m. Again, it is pointed out that strict silence must be maintained concerning the events at the camp. Extreme care must be paid to the camp equipment, so it can be returned without damage to its original function. Those found removing or damaging any kind of equipment will have to pay for replacements.

Quite obviously, the scheduled deportations to the East, start-ing in the fall and winter of 1941, could not have been accom-plished without precise logistical preparations. Even the procurement of enough rolling stock to transport 50,000 Jews must have been very difficult, since it coincided with the severe supply problems faced by the army now poised in front of Mos-cow. Despite the difficulties, the first wave of mass deportations was accomplished with near perfection. We know that RSHA and the National Railroad were in close contact. They held reg-ular conferences (e.g., July 10, 1942 in Bamberg) to fix timeta-bles for special trains, each carrying about 1,000 persons to the East. The destination of the trains was announced as Wolkow-ysk near Minsk. In reality this was a connection point to the extermination camp in Trostinec.

The assembly and time schedule of a train was painstakingly prepared and the financial responsibilities were clarified. The Gestapo requisitioned the trains. Fees were paid to the National Railroad, and the deportees themselves were charged 50 reich-marks for transportation costs. This sum had to be paid in cash at the assembly point. Further regulations required the escort troops to deliver the money to the appropriate state police office at the final destination. The sum to be handed over amounted to 50,000 marks per transport!

Details can be gathered from other sources, such as a May 1942 notice of the National Railroad in Vienna, for example, announcing the reduced one-way fare for special trains to Minsk of 20.20 reichmarks per person. One-way, or course, because trains to Minsk terminated either at one of the execu-tion sites or at the Trostinec extermination camp.

None of those forced to board the train at Nuremberg/Lang-wasser was aware of the real facts behind the deportations, because "No information about train schedules is to be given to outsiders and particularly to passengers on the special trains."

Certainly, the criminal police officer in Forchheim knew the schedule; but what he made of the fact that the destination was Riga is not known. On the train's departure, when the doors to the cars were locked, the passengers received the first inkling of the situation in which they were caught. As the train pulled out of Nuremberg, they peered out the windows, anxiously trying to guess which direction it would take, greatly disconcerted as it passed the Jewish cemetery, which seemed to be an ill omen.

There are several survivors' reports about the transport from Nuremberg to Riga. They all agree that conditions during the trip were very depressing. Only a few cars, located right behind the locomotive, were heated. Compartments intended for eight people were loaded with ten or twelve. To this was added all the hand luggage. Despite promises, no consideration was given to family groups. Even at the start of the journey to the East, family members were separated.

No supplies from the outside were available. Provisions taken along had to last the entire journey. Water was available only twice during the trip. A security police captain from Düsseldorf, who escorted one of the Riga transports at the beginning of December, left this account of a deportation:

> Confidential!
> Report of Evacuation of Jews to Riga
> Escort guard in the force of 1/15
> Dec. 11, 1941 to Dec. 17, 1941
>
> A. The course of the transport.
> The transport scheduled for Dec. 11, 1941 consisted of 1,007 Jews from the cities of Duisburg and Krefeld and a number of smaller towns and villages in the industrial area of Rhine/Westphalia. Düsseldorf was represented by only 19 Jews. The transport comprised Jews of both sexes and ranging in age from infants to 65 years.

The train was scheduled for 9:30 a.m. departure. The Jews were assembled on the loading platform at 4:00 a.m. Due to a shortage of personnel the National Railroad was unable to assemble the train so early, so that loading could only begin at 9:00 a.m. The boarding had to be done in great haste, because the railroad insisted on departure close to the scheduled time. This resulted in overcrowding in some cars. These circumstances created problems during the entire trip to Riga, because some of the Jews tried to reach the less-crowded cars. As time permitted, I gave permission to a few mothers, separated from their children, to change cars.

On the way from the stockyards to the loading platform a Jewish man tried to commit suicide by throwing himself in front of a streetcar. The car's cowcatcher was able to pick him up and he received only light injuries. At the start of the trip he pretended to be near death; after realizing that he could not evade his fate, he recuperated rapidly. Also, an older Jewish woman left the loading platform under cover of darkness and rain, fled to a nearby house, disrobed, and hid in a toilet. A cleaning woman discovered her there, and she was returned to the transport.

Loading the Jews into the cars was accomplished by 10:15 a.m. After several switching maneuvers, the train left the Düsseldorf/Derendorf freight yards around 10:15 a.m. in the direction of Wuppertal, a delay in departure of about one hour. After the last coupling of cars was completed, it was realized that the car carrying the escort troops (second class) was attached to the rear of the passenger cars, as the twenty-first car, instead of being in the middle of the train. Behind our car were seven freight cars loaded with baggage. The wrong positioning of the escort car caused the following disadvantages:

a. Due to a faulty heating system, there was insufficient pressure for the steam to reach the cars toward the rear of the train. Because of the extreme cold, the guards were not able to dry their wet clothes. (It rained during most of the trip.) I anticipated some sick calls among the troops.

b. The commanding officer was unable to oversee the entire train. Our searchlights were in good working order; but the distance to the first cars was too great to allow our guards to reach them at every stop. Furthermore, due to unexpected abrupt departures, they had trouble reaching the escort detail's car. At each stop at a railroad station the Jews immediately tried to contact other travelers to hand them mail or to ask for water. I decided to post two guards in a compartment of the first passenger car.

The rest of the trip continued as scheduled, passing the following cities: Wuppertal, Hagen, Schwerte, Hamm. Around 6:00 p.m. we reached Hannover/Linden. Here, the train remained for about one hour. I provided some of the Jews with water and also asked to have our car repositioned. It was promised, but at the last minute no locomotive was available to do the work. They notified the station in Stendal to make arrangements to fulfill my orders. The next stop was Misterhorst. There, at 9:00 p.m., car no. 12 was found to have an overheated axle. It was uncoupled, but no replacement car was available. The Jews affected had to be distributed among the other cars. The ensuing commotion was not to the liking of the Jews, many of them asleep. Some difficulties were encountered due to darkness and constant rain. Furthermore, the train was stopped outside the station, without the benefit of platforms. But with the proper force the situation was under control in a very short time. During the reloading our searchlights proved very useful. We arrived at the station in Stendal at 11:00 p.m. Here, the locomotive was replaced and an empty third-class car attached to the front of the train.

At 10:00 a.m., at the station in Pirchau, I had the station in Konitz alerted, asking for a one-hour stop on a siding to accomplish the following:

a. to relocate Jews into the empty car

b. to provide the Jews with water

c. to reposition the escort car

d. to receive refreshments from the Red Cross for our escort troops. . . .

At 5:15 a.m. [the following day], we arrived at the Laugszargen border station and 15 minutes later at Tauroggen station in Lithuania. The normal traveling time from here to Riga is 14 hours; but one-track roadbeds and the low priority of our train caused long delays at many stations. At Schaulen (1:12 a.m.), Red Cross sisters provided good and plentiful food to our escort troops: barley soup with beef. In Schaulen, Lithuanian railroad employees shut off the lights in all cars occupied by Jews. At the next station, I took the opportunity to allow the Jews, for the last time, to obtain water from a nearby fountain. . . .

At 7:30 p.m., we arrived at Mitau (Latvia). Here, we encountered considerably lower temperatures, snow drifts, and ensuing frost. Arrival at Riga was at 9:50 p.m. Here, the train was delayed for an hour and a half. We found out that the Jews were not to be sent to the Riga ghetto but to one in Shirotava, 8 kilometers northeast of Riga. On Dec. 13, at 11:35 p.m., after prolonged shunting back and forth, the train stopped at the military loading ramp at the railroad station in Shirotava. The train was without heat. Outside temperatures had fallen to -12° Celsius [7° Fahrenheit]. No replacement details of state police were on hand; therefore my men had to continue guarding the train. The train was officially handed over at 1:15 a.m. and six Latvian policemen took over the guard duties. It was after midnight, dark outside, and the ramp was covered with ice. So it was decided to unload the Jews and transfer them to the ghetto, 2 kilometers distant, on Sunday morning at daybreak. My escort troops were taken to Riga in two patrol cars provided by the security police. They were housed there for the night around 3:00 a.m. Quarters for me were provided in the inn requisitioned for the higher officers of the SS and police. . . .

The final destination of the transport from Nuremberg was also the freight yard of the railroad station in Shirotava, about 10 kilometers east of Riga. The conditions of the passengers could not have been much different from those described in the report on the Düsseldorf transport: ice, snow, and extreme cold. To this was added the bullying of the escort guards and the beatings by the SS troops awaiting the new arrivals. "The transport was delivered into the hands of SS Lieutenant Krause. He immediately asked for 'our King of the Jews,' referring to the Jew assigned to lead the transport. As soon as this man reported to Krause, he was hit over the head with a dog whip." So reads the report of a deportee from Würzburg. Someone else's description is: "After about three days we detrained at Shirotava, a village near Riga, where SS men welcomed us with beatings. We also heard gunfire." As a matter of fact a dentist from Nuremberg had already been shot to death by one of the guards at the train station. Next came the march to the camp at Jungfernhof (Jumpava Muiza), a few kilometers from Shirotava, on the Riga-Dünaburg highway. Originally a large estate, it had become a retreat for Soviet airmen. There were still a few barracks and some sheds left standing on the estate, all but sufficient to accommodate several thousand people in the winter. The economic and administrative divisions of SS headquarters planned to build an SS model farm there. An experienced farmer and SS squad leader, K.L.R., was in charge of the farm. At the beginning of the winter, he suddenly became commandant of a concentration camp. Since the first days of December, one transport after another of Jews from the Reich had been pouring into the camp, each transport comprising about 1,000 souls. The commandant of Jungfernhof was not the only one taken unawares; the responsible offices of the Reichskommissariat Ostland were also surprised. Nobody had counted on such speedy arrivals of transports, a situation which required fast improvisation to provide housing space, unless of course, the deportees were shot as soon as they arrived, as was the fate of a transport originating in the Reich that arrived in Kovno in November 1941. The security police commandant in Riga, Dr. Rudolf Lange, sent a letter, marked "secret," to Reichskommissar Heinrich Lohse (dated November 8, 1941):

> According to notification from Reich Security Service headquarters in Berlin, 50,000 Jews are scheduled to be deported to the Ostland. As mentioned, 25,000 Jews are destined for Riga and 25,000 for White Russia. . . .
> The construction of barracks near Salaspils has been accelerated. Since, due to difficulties in obtaining building materials and the shortage of skilled labor, the barracks will not be ready for the first transports, arrangements have been made to house the first deportees in the military barracks at Jungfernhof (to the right of the Riga-Dünaburg highway, between Riga and Salaspils). An agreement has been reached with the Riga-Land district commissioner, whose chief of staff, Party Comrade Bruhn, inspected the site. . . .

Around the same time, room was made for new arrivals in the Riga ghetto by summarily shooting the majority of the resident Jews. A deportee from Vienna, who was sent to the empty ghetto, reported finding apartments that gave the impression that the previous residents had just departed. Food, now frozen, had been left on the table, and everything looked lived-in.

We can imagine how things appeared at Jungfernhof when the transport from Nuremberg arrived there on December 2: unfinished buildings, unheated, barely fit for habitation; in the yards huge heaps of empty suitcases with the name tags of their former owners still attached; the remainder of a passing transport just transferred, most likely to Salaspils. The abandoned pieces of luggage led to the assumption that the deportees had been robbed of the greater part of their possessions. None of the building materials and tools everybody had been urged to take along was in sight. These items had quickly disappeared into other channels: the black market dealings and barter arrangements of the SS. People had to make do with things on hand. Dormitories were improvised, separating men and women; in the meantime, the camp population increased steadily. Still, nobody was aware that the transports from the Reich had landed in the center of activity of the Einsatzkommandos (extermination units). Latvia was the hunting ground of the bloodthirsty Einsatzkommando A. On December 31, 1941, the leader of the unit in Libau reported on its activities to the chief of the SS and police in Libau; his report will give us an idea of what was in store for those interned at Jungfernhof.

> Our aim at Commando #2, as envisioned from the very beginning, is a radical solution to the Jewish Question by executing all Jews. This has led us to wide-ranging mop-up operations in the entire area, implemented by special commandos with the help of hand-picked forces of the Latvian auxiliary police (mostly relatives of exiled or murdered Latvians). At the beginning of October, the approximate number of Jews executed in our zone of activity was 30,000. In addition, a few thousand Jews were eliminated by the [Latvian] self-defense units, on their own initiative, after the usual pep talk.
>
> The complete liquidation of all Jews in Latvia has not been possible, due to the economic situation, especially the requirements of the army. . . . However, by the end of October the Latvian countryside was completely purged.
>
> . . . At the beginning of November, only some 30,000 Jews were left in the Riga ghetto, 4,300 in Libau, and 7,000 in Dünaburg. After that time, 4,000–5,000 Jews were executed in connection with criminal prosecutions, such as failing to wear the Jewish star, black market activity, fraud, etc. In addition, Jews in the ghettos who were not fully able to work or

were of no other use were eliminated in the course of several extended actions. Thus, on Nov .9, 1941, 11,034 were executed at Dünaburg; at the beginning of December 1941, during an extensive operation ordered by a high official of the SS and police, 27,800 in Riga; and in the middle of December 1941, 2,350 Jews in Libau, at the request of the Reichskommissar. The remaining Jews (2,500 in Riga, 950 in Dünaburg, and 300 in Libau) were spared because they were highly skilled workers. . . . Since December 1941, transports from the Reich have been arriving in quick succession. So far, a total of 19,000 Jews have been deported to Riga. They are housed partly in the ghetto, partly in a temporary transfer camp, and partly in barracks at a newly established camp near Riga.

Only a few of the Jews from the Reich are able to work. 70% to 80% are women, children, and old men, not fit for work. The mortality figure of the evacuated Jews is steadily on the rise. Evidently, the old and feeble Jews are not able to survive the extremely harsh winter months. To prevent outbreaks of epidemics in the ghetto and at both camps, individual Jews infected by dysentery and diphtheria were isolated and executed. To conceal these measures from the local Jews and those in the Reich, the removal of the sick was disguised as a transfer to a Jewish old-age home or hospital. Mentally ill Jews were accorded the same treatment.

This monstrous text is a depraved mixture of secrecy and candor. The words used are "separation" as well as "execution" of the sick at Jungfernhof and "pep talk" to incite the Latvian self-defense units. Here we see individuals at work who, shamelessly and without inhibition, in language as well as in conduct, determined the fate of the uprooted Bambergers in their hands. The precipitous fall from relatively human living conditions in Bamberg, albeit restrictive and depressing, into the abyss of annihilation was frightening, terrifying, and cruel.

There is ample suspicion that the large transports in the fall and winter of 1941–42 had as their ultimate goal the complete disappearance of the Jews of the Reich in the far reaches of the East. Perhaps the idea of a mechanized, systematic destruction was not yet fully ripened, but the above-mentioned reports clearly show that the police authorities in Riga, as well as in other parts of Reichskommissariat Ostland, had few scruples about implementing the methods used on Latvian Jews and Jews from the Reich. It was only a matter of time until the Final Solution of the Jewish Question was in full operation.

Participants in the first extensive deportations were granted a brief stay of execution, but under what kind of living conditions? A woman from Nuremberg had this to say about her experiences in a deposition made after the war:

> Jungfernhof was a large estate. Men and women were housed separately. The women and children were sent to a larger building with a hayloft at the top and stables below. There we found bunks, three or four stacked one upon the other. About 600 women and children were crammed into this building. . . . The men were quartered in a similar large building, about 50 meters from ours. The men were allowed to visit the women's quarters during the day, in their off-hours. Women were also allowed to visit the men's quarters, but few took advantage of this, because of the extreme cold there. It was a very severe winter and the men's quarters were in a wooden building, while the women's quarters were of stone, at least on the lower floor. . . . Beginning in February 1942, the so-called transports started. First the mentally ill were removed. We had no inkling that they were to be killed. The rumor was that they were transferred to hospitals in Riga. This was followed by more transports, mostly of sick, old, and feeble people. Even these transports did not arouse suspicion.

It is human nature not to believe the worst. Good news and news with seemingly limited impact was easily believed, while bad news was rejected. The removal of the sick was bad news, but the fast-spreading gossip that they were being transferred to a clinic was readily accepted by the inmates.

> On March 26, 1942 a large transport left the camp. The camp elder [a Jew] told us that 1,700 people were deported. On the same day, a general roll-call was ordered. All inmates had to be accounted for. . . . Rumor had it that the transport was intended for the canning plants in Dünamünde. Believing this, nobody objected to the transport. As a matter of fact, some were quite cheerful, hoping for a better life at the canneries, especially as far as food was concerned.

Operation Dünamünde runs like a common thread through the entire oral history of Jungfernhof. Whether the survivors came from Würzburg, Stuttgart, or Vienna, it was a pivotal event, that bothered inmates in all the camps in the Riga area and caused great anxiety. Quite soon it became evident that the journeys on the army trucks did not terminate at a cannery, but at a forest called Bikiernki, Birch Grove.

> The transport of March 26, 1942 emptied our camp. Only about 450 people remained, mostly able-bodied workers. It took three to four weeks after the transport of March 26, 1942 for the real story to reach us: namely, that all the deportees were killed on the same day in a forest near Riga.
>
> I can't recall precisely how this news reached us at the camp. I remember that able-bodied inmates worked in the surrounding fields and must have had contact with local farmers. From them they received the news that all the deportees evacuated on March 26 were shot on the same day in a dense forest near Riga.

In another camp near Libau the bad news arrived sooner. The clothing of the murdered victims was returned to be used again. Inmates from Franconia were ordered to sort the clothes.

> My son, Max F., who eventually died during a bombing raid on Libau at the end of October 1944, told me that he and a few other inmates were ordered to unload trucks filled with the clothing of the executed Jews. In some of the coats he found I.D. cards belonging to our own acquaintances.

This from the account of a woman from Bayreuth, testifying before the Bayreuth County Court on procedures to obtain official death certificates of deportees.

The chain of events was as follows: Around Easter 1942 Reichskommissariat Ostland started wide-spread total-extermination operations against all Jews in its territory, whether native Jews or deported from the Reich. Even army and SS officers had trouble rescuing able-bodied workers needed for forced labor. How few were finally spared is shown, among other sources, by the statistics of the Jungfernhof camp. On March 20, 1942 the camp had 2,150 inmates. On March 26, about 1,700 were "selected"; this amounts to 79% of the entire camp population. There remained 450 people fit for heavy work. All sources agree unanimously that these numbers are correct.

The executioners made no attempt to keep their work a secret. All of Latvia was aware of the mass executions taking place during those weeks to which a large part of the deportees from Bamberg fell victim. Remarkable are the observations of a Riga housewife who lived not far from the Birch Grove:

> My house is located 1 to 1½ kilometers from the forest. I saw the people herded into the forest and I heard the shots. I know that the Germans murdered more than 10,000 people in the span of two days. It happened on Good Friday and Saturday before Easter 1942. The people arrived in buses and

other gray vehicles. They came in groups of four or five buses or trucks, at intervals of 30 minutes to an hour. The buses and vehicles were crammed with Jews. On those days, Friday and Saturday, they arrived day and night. On Friday alone, I counted 41 buses on the way to the forest in the span of 12 hours. Twenty to thirty minutes later, they left the forest empty. My neighbors and I heard shots from rifles and automatic weapons all day and night. The clothing of the executed was loaded on the returning vehicles. . . .

On Easter Sunday all was quiet. The weather was beautiful and sunny. I, my family, and many others took a stroll into the forest to look at the graves of the innocent victims who had been shot on the previous day.

My family and all the other families with us saw among all the graves one that was still open and filled to the brim with corpses. The corpses lay helter-skelter, without clothes or in their underwear. We could see that the murdered were women and children. Alongside the grave were puddles of blood, hair, severed fingers, brains, skulls, children's shoes, and other personal belongings. . . . Among the victims were Jews from abroad. We could deduce this from various items left laying around. Next to almost every grave was a fire pit in which the fascists had burned useless items.

In the ashes we saw the remains of burned clothing, such as buttons, buckles, eyeglass cases and frames, metal parts of ladies' handbags, wallets and change purses, among many other personal items. Near the fire sites, we found papers, photos, and passes. From those items we learned the places of origin of the victims; many pictures had a photographer's stamp on the back revealing the names of towns. It was possible to determine that the victims came from Austria, Germany, Hungary, and other countries.

The sources speak for themselves. We learn more than we like to know about the fate of the Jews from Bamberg "resettled" in the East. Of the 1,000 deportees who left Nuremberg on November 29, 1941, only eleven survived. Who was responsible for the events in Riga? The commandant of Jungfernhof was low in the chain of command and not up to the task of switching from manager of a model farm to commandant of a concentration camp with 2,000 inmates. In 1950, he was convicted of eight cases of murder and sentenced to life imprisonment. The courts did not hold him responsible for the "selection" or the transport to Dünamünde. We have to look somewhere else to place the blame. First in line are those who formulated the policies concerning the Jews in the Third Reich. They are well known. Next in line are the local bullies. They have to be held to account for the brutal and gory details of events taking place in Reichskommissariat Ostland. In Riga, two men come immediately to mind, the commander-in-chief of the SS and Police in Russia/North and Ostland, SS Major Friederich Jeckeln, and the security police commander in Latvia, SS Colonel Dr. Rudolf Erwin Lange.

Jeckeln admitted later that the policy of ethnic purity had as its goal the annihilation of undesirable ethnic groups. During his trial in Riga in 1945, he said:

> Himmler described my work in the Ostland as follows: To maintain quiet and order in the territories of the Ostland and White Russia and to eliminate to the last man all Jews in these areas. Himmler also mentioned other nationalities residing in the Ostland. He showed special hatred toward the Latvians, considering them an inferior race.

And who pulled the triggers? The members of Einsatzgruppe A, a part of the unit known as Einsatzgruppe of the Security Police and SD. Their task was a "special political police assignment" in the occupied territories in the East. This special assignment was part of the policy of ethnic purity, a euphemism for extermination of undesirable ethnic groups. The activities of these units are well documented. Their reports and the trail they left by their activities bring one to the conclusion that, in plain language, they were gangs of murderers.

7

The End of the Community

FOR THE JEWS OF BAMBERG, the gravity of the situation must have become clear after they saw the cruelties accompanying the first transport. What until recently had been mere rumors now turned into harsh realities. Acquaintances, friends, and relatives had disappeared into a black hole. Anxious and plagued by doubts, the Jews of Bamberg waited hopefully for signs of life. The wait was in vain, and they had to assume that the deportees had, in fact, met a terrible fate.

The activities of the Jewish communal administration were no help in raising hopes. The stream of anti-Jewish decrees did not dry up. On the contrary, it turned into a torrent. No week passed without new restrictions or humiliating new decrees touching on the most basic needs of daily life. A few days after the departure of the transport, on December 2, 1941, the remaining Jews received this notice:

Reichsvereinigung der Juden in Deutschland
Bavaria District
Bamberg Branch

Bamberg, Dec. 2, 1941

To community members and communal trustees in the surrounding counties:
1. In accordance with orders from the State Police, Depart-

151

ment P, Jews are not allowed to sell their assets or give
them away as gifts.
2. Typewriters in the possession of Jews must be registered
with the community office at once, including a report on
their make and condition. (This applies to Bamberg only.)
3. All front-line veterans of the 1914–18 World War must
report immediately to the community office. For the outly-
ing districts we have enclosed forms which must be completed and returned to our office.

sign. Dr. Siegmund Israel Bauchwitz
sign. Helene Eckstein

This document deserves closer scrutiny. At first glance, under
normal conditions of life, a reader might interpret the text as an
intimation of consideration and a chivalrous gesture toward old
war veterans. But he would be dead wrong! Those making the
rules reserved consideration and chivalry only for their own
kind. To arrive at a correct interpretation of the decree concerning war veterans one must read the ordinance of the Reichsmin-
istry of the Interior, dated December 18, 1941: "Jewish veterans
with severe war injuries, who by law are obligated to wear the
Jewish star, will from now on not receive documents issued to
major war casualties." We may remember that as recently as
1935, Jewish combat veterans were the recipients of a Citation
of Honor. But the concept of honor had long since changed,
and any kind of consideration was out of the question.

Even Death for the Fatherland was of little value as far as
Jews were concerned. Ulrich von Hasse recalls a remark that
Hitler made on November 1, 1941, in response to a question
about the treatment of Jews with war decorations: "Those swine
stole the medals." These words, uttered by the leader of the
regime, take on a poignant meaning in the light of the rumors
heard throughout the era of the Third Reich that Hitler's Iron
Cross First Class was a *Selbstauszeichnung* (i.e., a medal awarded

by one's own imagination). These rumors were fueled by the fact that Hitler's war records disappeared from the Munich war archives in the spring of 1933 and were later replaced by new files.

Need we examine further these abhorrent official pronouncements from those days? The answer is yes, if only to show the extent to which the authorities were capable of shedding the trappings of humane behavior. On December 12, 1941, a decree issued by Reich Security Service Headquarters (IV B 4 b-1244/ 41) prohibited the use of public telephones by Jews who were required by law to wear the Jewish star. Another decree from the same source, dated January 4, 1941 (it was found in a bulletin by the Gestapo in Darmstadt), reads as follows:

> In the framework of a drive collecting woolen clothing and furs for the Eastern Front, Jews must be urged to surrender all winter clothing suitable for use at the front. It must be made clear to the elders of the Jewish communities that the appearance of Jews in furs will provoke citizens of German blood; after all, people of German blood have willingly donated their winter clothing for use on the front lines. To avoid public raids, Jews are urged to surrender the clothing voluntarily. The district offices of the Reichsvereinigung are in charge of the collection.

Remember how difficult it was to outfit the deportees of the first transport from Bamberg with suitable winter clothing. Moreover, starting February 14, 1942, bakeries and cake shops were prohibited from selling cakes to Jews and Poles (note the combination of these groups), and to add insult to injury, signs to this effect had to be posted in the stores. On February 15, Jews were forbidden to keep house pets, and on February 17, they were prohibited from subscribing to newspapers or buying them from vendors. On March 16, they were forbidden to buy flowers, and finally, on April 24, they were ordered to surrender all shaving equipment and all unused combs and hair scissors to the "designated bureaus." The height of absurdity was reached with a regulation issued by the party chancellery banning the sale of German folk costumes to Jews and foreigners.

No traces are left of the community bulletins issued after the year 1941. Until then, relatively authoritative reports—firsthand information, as it were, on events concerning the community—are available. Afterwards, we must do without these sources. The lack of bulletins is by no means an indication that the communal administration ceased issuing communications of this type. After all, it was still the conduit for Gestapo activities and under Gestapo control. The fact is that none of the notices survived. Perhaps those who had preserved the previous source material were deported with the first transport to Riga.

We have to rely on a very thin file of administrative documents. Reconstructions of events lose the personal touch because the reports on the fate of Bamberg's Jews now emanate from third parties. The Bamberg municipal administration, probably at the behest of the Gestapo, registered all the remaining Jews after the large transport left the city on November 27, listing them by name, birth date, and residence. Marginal comments in inks of different colors and the lines drawn through many names lead to the conclusion that this was the master list of Bamberg's Jews, kept up-to-date by comparing it with Gestapo deportation rosters. All told, 126 Jews were left; they continued to live in the city, under the shadow of the unknown fate awaiting them.

JEWS RESIDING IN BAMBERG, DEC. 1, 1941[1]

1. Aigner, Bertha Sara, née Singer, born Jan. 6, 1887,

---

1 A number of handrwitten alterations were made to the original document. Here , deleetions are indicated by a line through a word and handwrritten items are given in italics.

Munich. ~~Plainserhof 20~~. *Zinkenwörth 17.*

2. Aron, Albert Israel, born Jan. 31, 1871, Zeckendorf [correction illegible].~~Herzog Max St. 3/I.~~ *Obere König St. 19/II.*

3. Aron, Berta Sara, née Freudenberger, born June, 9, 1890, Arnstein. Herzog Max St. 3/I. Obere König St. 19/II.

4. Ascher, Rosa Sara, née Hess, divorced. born Nov. 4, 1899, Bamberg. Augusten St. 18. (since Dec. 30, 1940, Bendorf, mentally ill)

5. Bamberger, Nanni Sara, née Neuburger, born July 26, 1869, Obereuerheim. Kessler St. ~~6a/I.~~ *15/II*

6. Bauchwitz, Dr. Sigmund Israel, born Nov. 13, 1876, Schwiebus. Hain St. 7/o.

7. Bauchwitz, Alice Sofie Sara, née Ehrlich, born Jan. 31, 1888, Bamberg. Hain St. 7/o

8. Baum, Justin Israel, born Sept. 24, 1893, Bamberg. Hindenburgplatz 2/I.

9. ~~Berg, Doris Sara, née Mayer, born June 19, 1857, Bayreuth. Zinkenwörth 2/I.~~

10. Berger, Moses, born ~~Aug. 15, 1895, Marburg,~~ *Apr. 9, 1877, [correction illegible]*. ~~Kettenbrück St. 4.~~ *Zinkenwörth 2/II.*

11. Berger, Ester Sara, née Gerstner, born Oct. 17, 1880, Cracow. ~~Kettenbrück St. 4.~~ *Zinkenwörth 2/II.*

12. Bernet, Babette Sara, née Kaltenbacher, born June 15, 1867, Adelsdorf. Luitpold St. 16/II.

13. Bernet, Hedwig Sara, born Sept. 19, 1890, Frensdorf. Luisen St. 6.

14. Bernet, Sofie Sara, née Mann, born June 14, 1863, Ermetzhofen. Luisen St. 6.

15. ~~Bettmann, Bernhard Israel, born Dec. 14, 1875, Weidnitz, Luisen St. 12/I.~~

16. ~~Bettmann, Bertha Sara, née Rosemann, born Oct. 3, 1883, Kronach. Luisen St. 12/I.~~

17. Bickart, Maria Sara, née Gutmann, born May 23, 1871, Lichtenfels. Friedrich St. 7/I.

18. Bleicher, Helene Sara, née Einzig, born Feb. 7, 1867, Cracow. ~~Kettenbrück St. 4.~~ *Zinkenwörth 2.*
19. Brand, Lina Sara, née Reiss, wife of brewer, born Nov. 16, 1881, Gross-Zimmern/Hesse. Härtlein St. 16. (Identified as *Volljude* on May 29, 1941.)
20. Brandes, Meta Sara, born Jan. 23, 1875, Rotenburg/Fulda. ~~Hain St. 4a/o.~~ *Zinkenwörth 2.*
21. Brandes, Maria Sara, born July 26, 1865, Mühlhausen. ~~Hain St. 20/I.~~ *Hain St. 14/II.*
22. ~~Brief, Markus Israel, born Aug. 13, 1895, Bamberg. Zinkenwörth 2.~~
23. ~~Brief, Regina, born Sept. 24, 1888, Hamburg. Zinkenwörth 2.~~
24. Brückmann, Fanny Sara, born May 19, 1875, ~~Bamberg,~~ *Kraisdorf.* Hauptwach St. 14/II.
25. Brückmann, Rosa Sara, born Nov. 28, 1869, Kraisdorf. Hauptwach St. 14/II.
26. Buchstein, Siegfried Israel, born Nov. 4, 1863. Nuremberg. Au St. 23/II.
27. Dehler, Irma Sara, née Frank, born Sept. 24, 1898, Steinach/Saale. Hain St. 21/I.
28. Dessauer, Julius Israel, born June 15, 1866, Bamberg. Hain St. 8.
29. Dessauer, Emilie Sara, née Arnold, born Nov. 6, 1874, Augsburg. Hain St. 8.
30. Dorn, Hermann Israel, born Sept. 11, 1865, Ermreuth. ~~Luitpold St. 48/II.~~ *Zinkenwörth 2.*
31. Dornfest, Luitpold, born Dec. 21, 1915, Bamberg. Luitpold St. 16/II.
32. Dornfest, Breindel Berta Sara, née Goldschneider, born Dec. 29, 1881, Cracow. Luitpold St. 16/II.
33. Eckstein, Helene Sara, born Jan. 31, 1893, Bamberg. Hain St. 7/o.
34. Ehmann, Sigmund Israel, born Feb. 5, 1866, Ullstadt. Friedrich St. 8/I.
35. Ehmann, Babette Berta Sara, née Heim, born Oct. 29,

1871, Würzburg. Friedrich St. 8/I.

36. Ehrlich, Max Israel, born Jan. 14, 1880, Bamberg. Herzog-Max St.3/II.

37. Ehrlich, Lina Sara, née Stein, born Feb. 9, 1888, Hesselhausen. Herzog-Max St. 3/II.

38. Ensminger, Gertrud Sara, née Brauer, born Aug. 30, 1884. Pschow. Weide 7.

39. Eschwege, Jakob Israel, born Dec. 23, 1875, Bamberg. Friedrich St. 8/I.

40. Eschwege, Selma Sara, née Baruch, born Mar. 5, 1889, Czempin. Friedrich St. 8/I.

41. Fleischmann, Elise Sara, née Wertheimer, born Mar. 20, 1865, Gunzenhausen. Friedrich St. 7/I.

42. Fleissig, Max Israel, born Aug. 22, 1877, Bamberg. Friedrich St. 8/o. *Generalsgasse 2.*

43. Freudenberger, Karl Israel, born May 12, 1868, Unterleinach. Herzog-Max St. 1. *Zinkenwörth 17.*

44. Freudenberger, Sidonie Sara, née Neuburger, born Feb. 11, 1879, Lauchheim. Herzog-Max St. 1. *Zinkenwörth 17.*

45. Freudenberger, Selma Sara, née Goldman, born Sept. 19, 1873, Bamberg. Herzog-Max St. 1. *Sofien St. 7/I.*

46. Fried, Betty Sara, née Bachmann, born Mar. 17, 1867, Kronach. Sofien St. 7/I.

47. Gerstner, David, born April 7, 1905, Bamberg. Kettenbrück St. 4/I.

48. Goldmann, Martin Israel, born Nov. 24, 1871, Bischberg. Franz-Ludwig St. 14.

49. Graf, Selma Elisabeth Sara, née Reichhold, born June 11, 1887, Nuremberg. Franz-Ludwig St. 15.

50. Grollmann, Fanni Sara, née Rosenstraus, born Mar. 16, 1864, Bamberg. Generalsgasse 2.

51. Grollmann, Johanna Sara, born Nov. 13, 1892, Regensburg. Generalsgasse 2.

52. Grünebaum, Moritz Israel, born June 28, 1879, Niederwerrn. Schützen St. 16/I/r.

53. Grünebaum, Sofie Sara, née Klein, born Jan. 9, 1875, Bamberg. Schützen St. 16/I/r.

54. Guth, Charlotte Sara, née Hirschmann, born Oct. 27, 1864, Gross-Kotzenburg. Kessler St. 18/II.

55. Hecht, Elise Sara, née Oesterlein, born Sept. 13, 1862, Fürth. Obere König St. 19.

56. ~~Heimann, Hannelore Sara, born Sept. 21, 1922, Bamberg. Luitpold St. 22/I. (Employed as household help).~~

57. Herrmann, Heinrich Israel, born Nov. 11, 1857, Trabelsdorf. Luisen St. 3/I.

58. Herrmann, Klothilde Sara, née Rosenthal, born May 2, 1865 Fürth, Luisen St. 3/I.

59. ~~Hesslein, Salomon Fritz Israel, born Aug. 22, 1876, Bamberg. Schützen St. 46/o.~~

60. ~~Himmelreich, Rosa Sara, née Hermann, born Jan. 21, 1877, Demmelsdorf. Franz-Ludwig St. 11/o.~~

61. ~~Himmelreich, Sali Lina Sara, née Schatz, born May 24, 1877, Bamberg. Luitpold St. 16/II.~~

62. ~~Karl, Heinrich Israel, born May 14, 1869, Walsdorf, Zinkenwörth 17/II.~~

63. ~~Koburger, Rosa Sara, born Sept. 24, 1882, Bamberg. Schillerplatz 10/o. Zinkenwörth 2/II.~~

64. Kohler, Paula Sara, née Ehrlich, born Nov. 1, 1887, Bamberg. Franz-Ludwig St. 10/II.

65. ~~Kohn, Karl Israel, born May 20, 1856, Burgkunstadt. Luitpold St. 40/II.~~

66. Kronscher, Josef Sigmund Israel, born May 24, 1881, Bamberg. Schützen St. 30.

67. Kupfer, Fritz Michael Israel, former merchant, born Feb. 23, 1881, Bamberg. Jakobsberg 17/O.

68. Kupfer, Leonie, Sara, née Heinemann, born Sept. 27, 1874, Rotenburg/Fulda. Sofien St. 7/I.

69. Kupfer, Semi, born Oct. 30, 1871, Bamberg. Sofien St. 7/I.

70. Leopold, Willy Israel, born July 26, 1878, Kleinlangheim. ~~Hain St. 8/o.~~ *Schützen St. 15/I.*

71. Lessing, Otto Israel, born May 12, 1875, Bamberg. Hain St. 7/I.
72. Lessing, Nelly Sara, née Ehrlich, born Oct. 25, 1886., Bamberg. Hain St. 7/I.
73. Lindner, Leopold Israel, born Oct. 1, 1902, Burgkunstadt. Sofien St. 0. At present in Eglfing/Haar.
74. Lipp, Ilse Sara, student, born Jan. 8, 1926, Bamberg, Single. Habergasse 1/I.
75. Löbl, Caroline Sara, née Schloss, born Aug. 23, 1861, Maroldsweisach. Hain St. 7/I
76. Lonnerstädter, Helen Sara, born Nov. 28, 1896, Mellrichstadt. Hain St. 7/o.
77. Marx, Hugo Israel, born Dec. 22, 1877, Bamberg. Franz-Ludwig St. 26/II.
78. Marx, Anna Sara, née Kronacher, born May 4, 1882, Bamberg. Franz-Ludwig St. 26/II.
79. Mattissohn, Heimann Israel, born Sept. 4, 1867, Wusen. Zinkenwörth 17/III.
80. Mayer, Frieda, née Stern, born Oct. 1, 1872, Fürth. Herzog Max St. 31/o. *Luitpold St. 16/II.*
81. Michels, Erich Israel, born Oct. 25, 1884, Schievelbein. Kessler St. 18/o.
82. Michels, Simon Israel, born Jan. 24, 1853, Regenwalde. Kessler St. 18/III.
83. Mosbacher, Kurt Israel, born May 20, 1907, Kronach. Friedrich St. 7/I.
84. Mosbacher, Ludwig Israel, born Jan. 23, 1874, Kronach. Friedrich St. 7/I.
85. Mosbacher, Luise Risl Sara, née Kamm, born Sept. 19, 1876, Oberheiduck. Friedrich St. 7/I.
86. Löwentritt, Getti, born April 2, 1878, Ebelsbach. Amalien St. 18/o.
87. Naumann, Fanny Sara, née Hess, born Jan. 15, 1874, Bischberg. Franz-Ludwig St. 26/I.
88. Neisser, Elsbeth Sara, née Silberstein, born Oct. 12, 1867, Waldenburg. Lagarde St. 41/II.

89. ~~Neuburger, Ernst Israel, born Mar. 31, 1888, Fürth.~~
    ~~Hain St. 20/I.~~
90. ~~Neuburger, Mina Sara, née Stein, born Aug. 25, 1879,~~
    ~~Rödelsee. Schützen St. 21/I.~~
91. Neumann, Albert Israel, born Jan. 2, 1872, Rauenthal.
    Kessler St. 18.
92. Obermeier, Meta Sara, née Nathansohn, born Jan. 21,
    1872, Gross-Rhüden. Maximilianplatz 14/II.
93. Oppenheimer, Meier Israel, born Jan. 30, 1863, Theil-
    heim. ~~StangSt. 5/I.~~ *Zinkenwörth 17.*
94. ~~Palm, Samuel, born Nov. 28, 1877, Düsseldorf. Kessler~~
    ~~St. 18/O.~~
95. ~~Palm, Emilie Sara, née Anspacher, born Mar. 22, 1885,~~
    ~~Delmenhorst. Kessler St. 18/O.~~
96. Reichmannsdorfer, Isidor, born Mar. 22, 1885, Lisberg.
    ~~Habergasse 1/I.~~ *Kessler St. 18/II.*
97. Reuss, Ida Sara, born Mar. 17, 1876, Ottensoos. Zinken-
    wörth 2/II.
98. ~~Reuss, Emma Sara, born July 23, 1877, Bamberg,~~
    ~~Zinkenwörth 2/II.~~
99. Rosenfeld, Nina Sara born April 20, 1875, Bamberg.
    Adolf-Hitler St. 18.
100. ~~Rossheimer, Hugo Israel, born sept. 29, 1871, Schwa-~~
     ~~bach. Heinrichsdamm 1/II.~~
101. ~~Rossheimer, Rosa Sara, née Kaufmann, born Feb. 2,~~
     ~~1881, Lauchheim. Heinrichsdamm 1/II.~~
102. Rossheimer, Max Israel, born Sept. 29, 1871, Schwa-
     bach. Heinrichsdamm 1/II.
103. Rossheimer, Emma Sara, née Iglauer, born July 4, 1875,
     Burgkunstadt. Heinrichsdamm 1/II.
104. ~~Saalheimer, Martin Israel, born Dec. 8, 1881, Bamberg.~~
     ~~Heinrichsdamm 1.~~
105. Schwerin, Rosa Sara, née Grollmann, born Jan., 23,
     1891, Regensburg. Generalsgasse 2/II.
106. Silbermann, Siegfried Israel, born May 21, 1873, Bam-
     berg. Franz-Ludwig St. 26/I.

107. ~~Steinberger, Hugo Israel, born May 21, 1873, Bamberg. Franz-Ludwig St. 26/I.~~

108. ~~Steinberger, Elsa Sara, née Bechmann, born Mar. 22, 1884, Bamberg. Hain St. 26/I.~~

109. Sulzbacher, Albert Israel, born Jan. 20, 1866, Bamberg. Sofien St. 12.

110. Sulzbacher, Fried Sara, née May, born Feb. 21, 1876, Meiningen. Sofien St. 12.

111. Sulzbacher, Ernst Israel, born Dec. 18, 1869, Bamberg. Luitpold St. 48/II.

112. Traub, Isidor, born Oct. 6, 1881, Trunstadt. ~~Josef St. 14b.~~ *Zinkenwörth 17.*

113. Wald, Lilli Sara, born June 13, 1870, Bamberg. Friedrich St. 8/o.

114. Wald, Rosa Sara, born May 28, 1869, Bamberg. Friedrich St. 8/o.

115. ~~Walter, Irma Sara, born Sept. 18, 1910, Bamberg. Luitpold St. 48/I.~~

116. ~~Walter, Sally, born Feb. 6, 1940, Bamberg. Luitpold St. 48/I.~~

117. ~~Walter, Rosa Sara, née Kohn, born Aug. 24, 1884, Burgkunstadt. Luitpold St. 48/II.~~

118. ~~Wassermann, Martha Sara, née Nathausen, born June 14, 1878, Stargard. Hain St. 4a.~~

119. Weil, Albert Israel, born Dec. 27, 1865 Lörrach. Schützen St. 21/I.

120. Weil, Sofie Sara, née Dornacher, born Feb. 25, 1885, Lörrach. Schützen St. 21/I.

121. Weil, Ruth Sara, born Feb. 28, 1923, Bamberg. Schützen St. 21/I.

122. Weilheimer, Sofie Sara, born April 13, 1871, Bamberg. ~~Luitpold St. 48/II.~~ *Schützen St. 16/I.*

123. Weissmann, Max Israel, born Nov. 14, 1871, Baiersdorf. ~~Herzog-Max St. 31.~~ *Sofien St. 7/I.*

124. Weissmann, Bertha Sara, née Braun, born April 5, 1873, Kunreuth. ~~Herzog-Max St. 31.~~ *Sofien St. 7/I.*

125. Wiesenfelder, Jeanette Sara, née Laubheimer, born Mar. 6, 1877, Hainsfurth. ~~Friedrich St. 6/I.~~ *Sofien St. 6/O.*
~~126. Wolf, Hanna Sara, born Mar. 20, 1870, Bamberg. Zinkenwörth 17/II.~~

At the so-called Wannsee Conference on January 20, 1942, attempts were made to transform long-standing procedures into an organized scheme, thereby laying the groundwork for the planned Final Solution of the Jewish Question. The general public, of course, was not aware of the decisions made at the conference, but the end results were soon to be seen.

The stream of deportations to the Baltic states in November–December 1942 ended before the planned number of Jews had been evacuated from the Reich. The legendary "Russian Winter" arrived in full force in December and with it difficulties encountered by the entire transportation system. Mass deportations of civilians to the East were out of the question, at least until the spring of 1942, considering the stress on the supply lines that provisioned the armed forces. But with the first sign of milder weather, even before the start of new offensive actions on the Eastern Front, Security Service Headquarters made the reluctantly postponed effort of *Entjudung* ("removal of the Jews") a priority item. Franconia was a part of the renewed effort, as can be seen from a report by the state police bureau in Nuremberg/Fürth:

> On Mar. 18, 1942, a meeting took place at the Nuremberg/Fürth office of the state police under the direction of Councilor Dr. Grafenberger. The topic was the renewed evacuation of Jews. It was announced that the Nuremberg/Fürth state police bureau will resume the deportation of Jews on Mar. 23, 1942. Because the Nuremberg/Fürth bureau is unable to supply the mandatory 1,000 Jews from the local area, 170 Jews from Würzburg will join the transport from Nuremberg on the above date. The Würzburg state police

bureau will deport an additional 1,000 Jews within the next fortnight.

Sources covering state police activities in Nuremberg/Fürth are scarce due to the destruction of all the relevant files at the end of the war. But documents found in the offices of lower-level administrative agencies, especially the local councils in the surrounding area, give some insights into the fateful events that took place in March 1942. In the Bamberg area, evidently, the transport scheduled for March 23 (it actually left March 24), which was mentioned in the report of the Nuremberg/Fürth state police, mostly affected Jews from the surrounding villages. Only 13 Bambergers are listed, against 74 from the surrounding district.

Brief, Markus, Habergasse
Brief, Regina, Habergasse
Ehrlich, née Stein, Herzog-Max St. 3
Ehrlich, Max, Herzog-Max St. 3
Grollman, Johanna, Generalsgasse 2
Himmelreich, née Schatz, Sali, Luisen St. 8
Lessing, née Ehrlich, Nelly, Hain St. 7
Lessing, Otto, Hain St. 7
Neuburger, née Stein, Minna, Hain St. 5
Palm, née Anspacher, Emilie, Luitpold St. 28
Palm, Samuel, Luitpold St. 28
Walter, Irma, Luitpold St. 48
Walter, Sally, Luitpold St. 48

The remaining deportees were from Aschbach (7), Hirschaid (20), Schesslitz (32), and Trabelsdorf (15); those listed as originating in Schesslitz were most likely from the historically renowned rural Jewish communities of Demmelsdorf and Zeckendorf.

The age breakdown of this transport is of interest. While the average age of the Bamberg deportees was 51.9 (despite the inclusion of the 2-year-old son of the home economics teacher, Irma Walter), which is in line with the age level of the November 1941 transport, the average age of the rural group was considerably lower: 39.5. Here is a breakdown for the different villages: Aschbach 48, Hirschaid 38.85, Schesslitz 40, Trabelsdorf 35.3. Obviously, in contrast to Bamberg, the remaining Jews in the villages and small towns, now caught in the round-ups, were of a younger age. How are these statistics to be interpreted? Perhaps the feeling of danger was more pronounced in the larger cities. And it may be, too, that Zionist aliyah activities (emigration to Palestine) were much more intensive there than in the rural communities.

After 1938, the emigration of younger people from the cities led to a rapid increase in the average age of the remaining communities. This fact was mirrored in the average age of the final deportations. The statistics of the Jewish community of Bamberg reflect the trend. Very few Jewish births were registered in the files of the state-accredited Bamberg Women's Hospital in the 1930s!

Source material covering the March 1942 transport is very scarce. We know that the preparations followed the patterns established in November 1941: submission of a detailed declaration of assets, round-up by security police, luggage search at the White Dove, and finally, departure under police escort to the Nuremberg/Langwasser assembly camp. This was the start of the eastbound journey to the Generalgouvernement, terminating at Izbica, a point east of Lublin.

Four weeks later, additional Jews from the rural districts of Franconia were deported. Very little is known about the part played by Jews from Upper Franconia in this transport. Existing files give the impression that the center of activities was in Mainfranken (the region of Franconia along the Main River). Upper Franconian Jews were only apprehended to fill the mandatory quota of 1,000 deportees. Seven people came from Bamberg:

> Bettmann, Bernhard, Heinrichsdamm 1
> Rossheimer, Hugo, Hain St. 4a
> Rossheimer, née Kaufmann, Hain St. 4a
> Saalheimer, Martin, Heinrichsdamm 1
> Steinberger, née Bechmann, Else, Schützen St. 9
> Steinberger, Hugo, Schützen St. 9
> Wolf, Hanna

There were four men and three women whose average age was 57.2. Hanna Wolf, at age 20, was the youngest. Three persons were listed as "evacuated" in the Bamberg Registrar's Office as of March 30, 1942. They were: Anna Marx, née Kronacher (Franz-Ludwig St. 26), Hugo Marx (Franz-Ludwig St. 26), and Erich Michels (Kessler St. 18). Whether they were part of the above deportation cannot be determined because the official roster of the transport has disappeared.

As far as the transport itself is concerned, a detailed report can be found in the State Archives in Würzburg, compiled by the escort officer, an assistant chief of the Würzburg criminal police.

> The transport left the Würzburg central railroad station on April 25, 1942 at 3:30 p.m. It traveled through the following stations:
> April 25, 1942: Bamberg (loading of additional 103 Jews), Lichtenfels, Kronach, Saalfeld.
> April 26, 1942: Sagan, Glogau, Neulauba, border point, Lissa, Ostrowa, Schieratz, Zdunska, Lask, Pabia/Nitza, Kalisch.
> April 27, 1942: Tomaszoc, Konskie, Towanowice, Nieklan, Skarzyska, Radom, Pionki, Nastawina, Deblin.
> April 28, 1942: Lublin (arrival at 2:30 a.m., departure at 5:00 a.m.), Krupicem, Rejowiece, Krasnystaw (arrival at 8:45

a.m. and transfer of transport into the hands of Lieutenant Buhl of the Lublin state police office).
The full complement of deportees was handed over. There
were no disturbances. No police intervention was needed.
I returned to Würzburg on May 5, 1942 at 4:30 a.m. I
reported my arrival immediately, via telephone, to the night
duty officer at the bureau.

Krasnystaw and Izbica are situated east of Lublin, in an area
that late became the site of the first real extermination camps,
Belzec and Sobibor. At the beginning of May 1942 they were in
a preparatory phase; the methods of mass destruction of human
beings were still in the research-and-development stage. Considering this, we may deduce that the two transports from Franconia were not immediately led to slaughter, but were interned
in ill-equipped primitive ghettos, such as Izbica.

Strangely, signs of life of these transports reached Würzburg
and Nuremberg in the form of postcards. Of course, most of the
communications did not reach their intended recipients, but
were found in Gestapo files after the war. Here is a card from
Bernhard Rindsberger of Marktbreit:

> Dear Folks:
>   We are all well. Please send Paul and me a weekly allow-
> ance, as well as underwear, clothes, and food.
>   Greetings,
>   Bernhard

The card is postmarked Izbica, March 31, 1942, and therefore
was posted shortly after the transport's arrival at its final destination.

On April 23, 1942, Selma Baumann wrote to Würzburg:

> To the administration of the Jewish Home, Würzburg.
>   We sincerely beg you to send us gift parcels. We are
> allowed to receive packages and money, but we poor

Würzburgers have not seen any yet. The packages may weigh up to 4 kilo. We ask for soup concentrates and cubes and . . . [illegible], all in small quantities. We would also appreciate some cheese. We send regards to all of you. My dear husband does not feel very well. Again, heartiest greetings to you all from Selma.

The following comments by the Würzburg branch office of the state police were attached to the card:

> The enclosed card was submitted by SS Captain Merder of Würzburg SD headquarters. Please take no action. A number of letters and cards of this type were confiscated and reported to the Nuremberg/Fürth state police bureau, with a request to stop correspondence of this kind.

In the meantime, a number of cards reached addressees in Nuremberg. They were written by Miri Blumenthal, 18 years old, in Izbica and sent to an acquaintance in Nuremberg.

> Lublin, April 4, 1942
>
> Dear Dolfi!
> We arrived in good health and found work. How are you, the Hamburgers, and the Sahlmanns? Did you get my card from Izbica? If possible, send us money and food; we are allowed to receive unrestricted quantities. There are a lot of young people among us. Do you see Curt? Best regards and kisses.
>
> Miri, Josi

Another card, dated July 9, 1942, shows the return address of the sender as: Miri Blumenthal, Izbica/Wierpz, Block 2/230, District Lublin, Generalgouvernement.

The contents of the correspondence arouse suspicion, especially the choice of formal expressions like "arrived in good health" and "found work." One is left with the impression that we are dealing here with dictated texts, as was also the case with some of the communications from Auschwitz. There was a suggestion of relative well-being to be communicated to those still back home and to the world at large! The phrase "in unrestricted quantities" accompanying the request for packages can be discounted, as may clearly be seen in the following memorandum from an office of the Würzburg criminal police:

> According to a bulletin from the Nuremberg/Fürth state police bureau, Reich Security Service Headquarters will prevent any postal or freight traffic between Germany and the Generalgouvernement, or vice versa.

This memo is dated May 15, 1942. It is open to question whether any of the deportees from Franconia to Izbica were still alive at the end of 1942. In the summer and fall the mechanized destruction of human beings started, especially in the area of Lublin, at the three camps mentioned above. We must conclude that the transports from Franconia were among the first to fall victim to these atrocities. None of the deportees of the March and April 1942 transports ever returned.

It is almost impossible today to visualize the fate of the remnants of Bamberg Jewry after the initial deportations in November 1941. On top of the worries over "emigrant" friends and acquaintances and an extremely severe winter with a shortage of fuel and a lack of winter clothing, came the two transports in the spring of 1942. These deportations mainly affected Jews from the rural districts of Upper Franconia, but the tragedy took place under the eyes of Bamberg's remaining Jews. The White Dove—community center, place of worship, and seat of the administration—was again the assembly point where deportees were processed. This was a clear indication of what was in store for what was left of the Bamberg Jewish community. Illusions about a pioneering life in the East had long since given way to a deep anxiety that was constantly fed by the trickle of rumors. An elderly woman remarked to an Aryan acquaintance that she was willing to die without complaining, "but not like this . . ."

Some of the non-Jewish citizens of Bamberg still have memories of the year 1942. A woman now in her seventies recalls the departure of trucks from the Schönleinsplatz via Sophien Street to the railroad station. Happening to pass by on her bicycle, she saw people being loaded like cattle, with shouts and brute force. Her first reaction was to send a personal letter to Hitler, telling him that this kind of treatment was inhuman and undignified.

Another Bamberg woman, slightly older than the above-cited witness, remembers the departure of a transport from the White Dove. A puppy accompanied an elderly lady to the bus. After its mistress boarded the bus, it waited on the sidewalk. When the bus began moving, it ran alongside until it was out of breath, then started to howl loudly. This is a touching story, even after more than forty years, but it also has some typical characteristics, story elements so old that they are now stereotypes: the faithful animal mourning the fate of its mistress. Yet the story is more than another repetition of an old formula. The woman would not have recounted the heart-rending tale if she had not herself been deeply moved and disturbed by what she had witnessed. She did not dare to articulate her own dismay, so she used the cliché of the mourning animal. Man had to be silent, but a dumb animal could protest.

Some acts of spontaneous help must have occurred. Here is a story told by a peasant woman in her eighties from Friesen. She occasionally surreptitiously brought bread, even a pullet, to an old acquaintance from Buttenheim, now quartered at the White Dove. For these deeds she was denounced by the local Nazis back home. Among those condescendingly called "plain folks," a shred of communal solidarity remained, despite the incessant barrage of propaganda and hate.

In all likelihood, Bamberg was no different from any other place in the land. For most people, the fate of the Jews was not a cause for misgivings, let alone, protest. As Ian Kershaw concluded—and this applies to Bamberg as much as to the rest of the country—German reactions cannot be blamed only on intimidation but must also be attributed to indifference. The populace had little empathy with the fate of the minuscule remainder of the Jewish minority that was now being deported.

The end of Bamberg Jewry was heralded by a notice to the members and trustees of the community:

> As an addendum to our last bulletin concerning emigration note the following details, which we ask you to convey to all other members of the community:
>
> I. Evacuation from Bamberg will take place from the White Dove. Exact time is still unknown, but is expected to be in the first week of September. Destination: Theresienstadt.
> You must attend to the following preparations:
> (a) Settlement of all outstanding debts.
> (b) Every person must deposit 60 reichmarks in special account W at the bank of Wunder, von Wendland & Co., Bamberg. At the destination 50 reichmarks will be returned to you.
> (c) Arrears in dues owed to the Reichsvereinigung must be submitted to the branch office in Munich. The same applies to dues for the *Jüdische Pflicht* [Jewish duties].
> (d) Twenty-five percent of your cash (securities not included) must be deposited in special account W at Wunder, von Wendland & Co. before departure, to cover the shortfall created by indigents.
> (e) Every emigrant in possession of more than 1,000 reichmarks in liquid assets after complying with directions (a)–(c)

must sign a purchase contract for his stay in Theresienstadt. The amount of the purchase price is calculated as follows:

(1) Initial fee per person, 2,000 reichmarks.

(2) For each month up to the age of 85, 150 reichmarks 150 (5 years minimum).

Example: Husband born Mar. 25, 1860, wife born May 9, 1870.

For the husband, 5 years = 5 x 12 x 150 = 9,000 reichmarks.

For the wife, 12 years 9 months = 153 x 150 = 22,950 reichmarks. The initial fee must be paid with liquid assets, including life insurance policies with cash value and family insurance with redemption options (if unknown, allocate two-thirds of accumulated contributions). You must request the *payment of the redemption value* at once, with an order to pay the resulting sums directly to the account mentioned below.

(3) Due to the Reichsvereinigung's obligation to finance the purchase cost for indigent people, those with liquid assets remaining after they meet their own obligations are urged to contribute additional sums to cover the cost of the assistance. Guidelines set by the Reichsvereinigung, with the permission of the regulatory authorities, are as follows:

up to 50,000 reichmarks—50%

50,000 to 100,000 reichmarks—60%

100,000 200,000 reichmarks—75 %

over 200,000 reichmarks—90% of the liquid assets

(4) Payments as listed above can be made from the following accounts without special permission: restricted secured accounts in the category RdErl. RWM No. 60 of Aug. 8, 1940; also liquid assets with restricted access as per regulations of Dec. 1, 1940; also securities in Jewish hands, as defined in the Reich Commerce Department ordinance of July 21, 1942.

All payments to be made to special account W at the bank of Wunder, von Wendland & Co., Bamberg, either directly or by transfer.

II.*Luggage:* Only hand luggage and suitcases are permitted.

Hand luggage: Field bags, handbags, and knapsacks.

Suitcases: Hand-held cases with working locks.

Take the following items: sturdy shoes, clothing, and underwear, all in good condition.

Mark your luggage and suitcases with your name or securely attached baggage tags.

In addition, bring provisions for two days; also a cup or mug, a

1- to 2-liter pot (all unbreakable), a big and a small ladle, and a set of table cutlery. Do not include fragile items, liquids, matches, or other inflammable items.

sign. Dr. Siegmund Israel Bauchwitz
sign. Helene Sara Eckstein

What immediately attracts our attention in this ominous bulletin is the ready use of euphemisms and code-words adopted from the regime's official terminology. We hear about "emigration" and "destination: Theresienstadt"; the emigrant is being "evacuated." At first glance, these are harmless words; but on a second reading the underlying menace becomes evident, despite the attempt at concealment. The language of the "authorities" comes through: "You must attend to the following preparations . . . You must deposit . . ."—orders and regulations that leave no doubt as to what your obligations are in the last days of your civilized existence.

The forced purchase contracts were an outright deception by means of which the Gestapo brazenly plundered any remaining Jewish assets and at the same time circumvented the Reich Finance Ministry so as to fill its own coffers. A check of the Finance Ministry's records reveals that the departments in charge of the liquidation of Jewish assets were left with almost worthless household objects which were handed over to the NSV (Nazi welfare organization) for a nominal price. Cash, insurance proceeds, and securities ended up in the coffers of the SS.

It goes without saying that the deportees did not receive the promised 50 reichmarks on arrival. Nor did they find anything resembling a community for senior citizens at their destination.

One thousand Jews from Franconia were assigned to the September 9, 1942 transport to Theresienstadt, among them about 200 each from Bamberg and Würzburg. A look at the final tally of deportees makes it clear that it was increasingly difficult to fill the mandatory quotas; the Jewish communities had shrunk considerably after the deportations in the fall of 1941 and the spring of 1942.

Again, the White Dove was the assembly point, but in contrast to both the spring transports, Jews from the city of Bamberg constituted the majority, in this case 54 people. The average age was 70.7 years (16 men, average age, 72.5; 38 women, average age, 69.0). It was the turn of Bamberg's Jewish elderly. In the fall of 1941, they had been spared the fate of deportation because ability to perform work was still a criterion for selection. Now the age range was from 46 (Helene Lonnerstadter, Kessler St. 18) to 89 (Simon Michels, also Kessler St. 18). The deportees from the surrounding districts were also considerably older than those in previous transports. The victims from the entire Bamberg district (a complete roster of the transport is on hand) averaged 62.5 years old.

The deportation of the elderly was the final episode in the long history of Franconian Jewry. During those last days they lived crammed into overcrowded, dilapidated housing in the villages, and often were expelled to Bamberg, where the White Dove was turned into an old-age asylum for Jews from the surrounding area. The Bamberg registrar compiled two lists in

1942, and the breakdown shows the location of the areas affected.

On Jan. 26, 1942 the following Jews from Bayreuth arrived in Bamberg:

127. Fleischmann, Karl Israel, former farmer, born Oct., 29, 1867, Aufsess, widower. Zinkenwörth 17.
128. Klein, Berthold Israel, former lawyer, born May 26, 1875, Bayreuth, married. Zinkenwörth 17.
129. Klein, Regina Sara, née Buff, born Dec. 16, 1881, Munich, married. Zinkenwörth 17.
130. Oppenheim, Henriette Sara, née Olzinger, born May 3, 1876, Windsbach, widow. Zinkenwörth 17.
131. Steinhäuser, Max Israel, former merchant, born Oct. 6, 1863, Burgkunstadt, married. Zinkenwörth 17.
132. Steinhäuser, Mina Sara, née Heumann, born Jan. 22, 1871, Rothenburg/Tauber, married. Zinkenwörth 17.
133. Sündermann, Rafael Israel, former cattle dealer, born May 14, 1874, Gerolshofen, married. Zinkenwörth 17.
134. Sündermann, Pauline Sara, née Fleischmann, born July 29, 1877, Oberlangenstadt, married. Zinkenwörth 17.
135. Ullmann, Lilli Sara, no occupation, born April 5, 1872, Sedan, France, single. Zinkenwörth 17.
136. Weinberger, Josef Israel, former merchant, born Mar. 14, 1861, Wüstensachsen, married. Zinkenwörth 17.
137. Weinberger, Rosette Sara, née Badmann, born Aug. 5, 1865, Oettingen, married. Zinkenwörth 17.

On April 20, 1942 arrived from Hirschaid:
138. Stein, Selma Sara, née Dingfelder, born May 20, 1891, Uhlfeld, widow. Zinkenwörth 17.

On April 28, 1942 arrived from Burgkunstadt:
139. Steinbock, Ignatz Israel, former sexton, widower, born Sept. 29, 1868, Lubanek near Leslau. Zinkenwörth 17.

On April 29, 1942 arrived from Kronach:
140. Bamberger, Theodor Israel, no occupation, single, born May 21, 1870, Friesen. ~~Zinkenwörth 17.~~ *Zinkenwörth 8/ 0.*

On June 23, 1942 arrived from Munich:
141. Neugebauer, Eugen Israel, cook, married, born May 21, 1904, Cologne/Rhine. Zinkenwörth 17.
142. Neugebauer, Else Sara, née Backes, born Feb. 11, 1905, Vervier, Belgium. Zinkenwörth 17.
143. Neugebauer, Manfred Israel, born Nov. 1, 1933, Düsseldorf. Zinkenwörth 17.

On June 30, 1942 arrived from Berlin:
~~144. Benger, Elfriede Sara, single, nurse, born Oct. 22, 1882, Kattowitz. Zinkenwörth 17.~~

On July 11, 1942 arrived from Forchheim:
145. Sundheimer, Berta Sara, single, no occupation, born Nov. 10, 1873, Mittelweissenbach. Zinkenwörth 17.

On June 15, 1942 arrived from Trabelsdorf:
146. Katz, Fanny, Sara, née Ullmann, born July 27, 1869, Trabelsdorf. Zinkenwörth 17.

The listing of the last-known official address of Jews registered in Bamberg yields the information that very few were taken from Zinkenwörth 17, the White Dove. The White Dove was by no means the residence of most of Bamberg's Jews; in other words, it was not a mini-ghetto. As a matter of fact, Jews continued to live in private apartments, often in Jewish-owned houses and often under the same roof with Aryan tenants. Hence, the "evacuations," mostly under police escort in the early morning hours, would not have been a secret to the fellow citizens who were their neighbors.

The modus operandi followed the well-established routine: pick-up at the residence, after the head of household completes and submits the declaration of assets; searches at the assembly point; acceptance of a declaration (for a fee!) that all assets are now the property of the Reich; surrender of all personal documents; and finally, transfer to the railroad station, where a special train is ready for their arrival. A directive for the assembling of such a train (for September 9, 1942), issued by the National Railroad Directorate in Nuremberg, survived the war.

> Re: Evacuation of 1,000 Jews from Nuremberg, Bamberg, and Würzburg on train no. Lp1511 and Da512 on September 10, destination Theresienstadt
>
> 1. This time, onloading of Jews and their baggage will not take place at Nuremberg/Märzfeld but at Nuremberg/Viehhof [the stockyards] on the manure-loading platform, Finken St. 33. Jews from Bamberg and Würzburg—approximately 200 each—to be onloaded in their respective cities. Empty cars for this purpose to be taken from train Lp1511 and routed to Bamberg and Würzburg. When loaded, these cars are to be returned to the Nuremberg switching yard.
> 2. Empty train Lp1511 will be directed to the Nuremberg switching yard (instead of Märzfeld) on September 20. Loaded train Da512 will leave the Nuremberg switching yard (instead of Märzfeld) at 6:14 p.m.
> 3. On September 9, three passenger cars from train Lp1511 will leave for Bamberg on train Dg6809, arriving at 4:35 p.m., to pick up the Bamberg Jews; four passenger cars from Lp1511 will leave the Nuremberg switching yard for Würzburg on De5061 at 10:09 p.m., to arrive at the Würzburg Central Station at 12:39 a.m. on September 10. A freight car will be added at the Würzburg station. At 9:38 a.m. on September 9, the remaining thirteen passenger cars of Lp1511 will arrive at the Nuremberg switching yard to be coupled with five freight cars and one "R" car

(for the escort personnel). This train to be ready to receive the Nuremberg Jews and their baggage at the manure-loading platform around 5:00 p.m. on September 9, if at all possible.

4. At 1:10 p.m. on September 10, three loaded cars will leave Bamberg with train De5144 for the Nuremberg switching yard, to arrive 3:39 p.m. At 11:13 a.m. on September 10, five cars will leave Würzburg Central Station with train Dg6456 for the Nuremberg switching yard, to arrive 4:04 p.m.

5. The assembled Nuremberg train at the manure-loading platform—eighteen cars plus one "R" car (including freight cars)—will leave around 5:00 p.m. for the switching yard to form train Da512. There the cars from Bamberg and Würzburg will be attached, passenger cars and freight cars in separate groupings. Da512 will leave the switching yard at 6:14 p.m. for Theresienstadt via Schnabelwaid-Hof.

 sign. F.

Even in hell order must prevail! The above document is proof of the National Railroad's desire to follow punctiliously the wishes of Security Service Headquarters; to complete their tasks conscientiously, paying attention to every detail. "Da" was the railroad's internal code for trains assembled to take German Jews to the East. Transports from other countries had different designations. Trains from Theresienstadt to Auschwitz were coded "Vd" for *Volksdeutsche*, "PJ" for Polish Jews, and, as seen above, "Da" for Jews from the Reich.

We ask the same question that H. G. Adler raised: What did the officials at the National Railroad Directorate think when they encountered the names Theresienstadt and Auschwitz?

One of the passengers on train Da512, which left Nuremberg at 6:12 p.m. on September 10, 1942, was the head of the Bamberg Jewish community, Dr. Siegmund Bauchwitz. Left behind to deal with the "final liquidation of business" was Helene Eckstein. In 1943 she was deported via Fürth to Auschwitz, also the final destination of the Bamberg Jews in Theresienstadt. They were deported sometime in 1943, on trains shamelessly and derisively dubbed "Family Transport," from the "senior" ghetto of Theresienstadt to the Auschwitz extermination camp.

On the very same day that the transport departed, Karl Bezold, chief organizer of the deportations, wrote the following letter to an acquaintance at the front:

> Dear Mr. L.:
> I have received your delightful letter. Many thanks. How touching that even at the front you think about your civilian occupation. I have fulfilled my previously made promises and accumulated quite a few old but beautiful objects. I wish you would return soon, so that I would be able to get rid of the lot. I don't have the space.
> Today, September 10, 1942, I evacuated the last 125 Jews; now we are free!
> Dear Mr. L., we are in good health. Give the damn Russian rabble a good thrashing and return quickly; there is a lot of new work waiting for you. All the best and sincere greetings from the homeland. Heil Hitler!
> Yours truly,
> Bezold

The "civilian occupation" of the recipient of this letter was a dealership in antiques. We can deduce that the "old but beautiful objects" were items belonging to Jews, now finding their way into commercial channels.

Other items followed the route laid down by the law to benefit the Reich treasury; real estate, for example, but also "old but beautiful objects" like paintings. The list compiled by the Bamberg Finance Department is reproduced in Appendix 2.

Decisions about the fate of racially mixed persons were still in dispute. No consensus was reached on the ultimate disposition of this group within the framework of the Final Solution. Doctrinaire Nazi purists wanted to eradicate all traces of Jewish blood in the German people. On the other hand, while pragmatists also wanted to preserve the dominance of German hereditary traits, they advocated the exemption of racially mixed people from the fate of the Final Solution.

The dispute between these two opinions found expression in a variety of propositions, memoranda, and even decrees issued by the authorities. One result of the difference in opinion was the creation of a category called "privileged mixed marriage." However, an influential clique saw these diversions as nothing but a lamentable softening of the race doctrine and made an all-out effort to have their position implemented. This meant that the offspring of first-degree mixed marriages, i.e., of marriages where one partner was *Volljude*, were condemned to deportation and extermination.

A notice from Nuremberg/Fürth state police headquarters, dated January 25, 1944, shows the change to a stricter policy in regard to *Mischlinge* (the offspring of mixed marriages). It was sent to the lord mayors of the cities of Ansbach, Bamberg, Bayreuth, Coburg, and Erlangen.

II B 4 Mo/Ap Jan. 25, 1944

> Re: Apprehension of Jews and Jewish *Mischlinge* of the first degree
> Encl.: None

> I respectfully request the complete files on Jews and first-degree Jewish *Mischlinge* now residing in your jurisdiction.

> I.A.
> N.N.

The Bamberg municipal administration compiled a list of Jews still residing in the city and forwarded it to Nuremberg/ Fürth on February 21.

> Submitted on Feb. 21, 1944 to the secret state police in Nuremberg.

> Identification of Jews and First-Degree Jewish *Mischlinge*[2] Residing in Bamberg

> a. Jews
> Blum, Justin Israel, advocate, born Sept. 24, 1893, Bamberg, married (wife non-Jew). Hindenburgplatz 2.
> Branco, Yenni, née Simonsohn, born Feb. 20, 1876, Berlin, married (husband non-Jew). Hain St. 28. (Injured in air raid in Hamburg).
> Brand, Karoline Sara, née Reiss, born Nov. 16, 1881, Gross-Zimmern, married (husband non-Jew). Hain St. 21.
> Dehler, Irma Sara, née Frank, born Sept. 24, 1898, Steinach-Saale, married (husband non-Jew). Hain St. 21.
> Ensminger, Gertrude Sara, née Brauer, born Aug. 30, 1884, Pschow/Upper Selisia, widow (husband was non-Jew). Weide 7.
> Fleissig, Max Israel, merchant, born Aug. 22, 1877, Bamberg, divorced (wife non-Jew). Generalsgasse 2.
> Grünebaum, Moritz Israel, merchant, born June 28, 1879, Niederwerrn, married (wife non-Jew). Schützen St. 16.
> Kohler, Paula Sara, née Ehrlich, born Sept. 1, 1887, Bamberg, married (husband non-Jew). Franz-Ludwig St. 10.
> Kronscher, Josef Israel, merchant, born Feb. 24, 1881, Bamberg, married (wife non-Jew). Schützen St. 30.
> Kupfer, Fritz Michael Israel, merchant, born Feb. 23, 1881, Bamberg, married (wife non-Jew). Jakobsberg 12.
> Leopold, Willy Israel, wine merchant, born July 26, 1878,

---

2 The offspring of two Jewish parents.

Kleinlangheim, married (wife non-Jew). Schützen St. 16.

Schwerin, Rosa Sara, née Grollmann, born Oct. 23, 1891, Regensburg, widow (husband was non-Jew). Generalsgasse 2.

Above-listed Jews have German citizenship.

b. First-Degree Mischlinge

Bonfig, Elisabetha, stenographer, born July 7, 1914, Bamberg, single. Juden St. 12/I.

Brand, Dorothea, seamstress, born Aug. 27, 1909, Worms, single. Härtlein St. 16.

Brand, Friedrich, journeyman carpenter, born Oct. 5, 1907, Worms, married. Neuerb St. 47/I.

Ensminger, Kurt, clerk, born Jan. 21, 1906, Doulevant le Chateau, married. Weide 7/I.

Haffner, Elsa, née Herz, born Jan. 22, 1899, Cologne, married. Herzog-Max St. 12/III.

Hamburger, Elisabeth, volunteer, born Aug. 5, 1914, Munich, single. Sophien St. 10/o.

Heilmann, Wolfgang, graduate student, born April 20, 1914, Güstrow, single, Schützen St. 30/II.

Helmreich, Rosa, née Rank, born Aug. 27, 1912, Altenstein nr. Ebern, married. Verdun St. 14/I.

Hesslein, Irmengard, born Jan. 12, 1913, Bamberg, single. Grüner Markt 8/II.

Hetz, Karolina, née Heindl, born Mar. 9, 1888, Nuremberg, married. Siechen St. 18/I.

Hock, Margareta, née Fleissig, born Sept. 25, 1903, Schweinfurt, married. Geyerswörth St. 8/I.

Katzenberger, Karl, born June 21, 1929, Bamberg, single, Geisfelder St. 117a.

Kohler, Elisabeth, assistant photographer, born Dec. 16, 1927, Bamberg, single. Franz-Ludwig St. 10/I.

Kohler, Rudolf Georg, student, born Mar. 31, 1925, Bamberg, single. Franz-Ludwig St. 10.

Kupfer, Karl, deacon, born Mar. 29, 1919, Nuremberg, single. Heinrichsdamm 32.

Kupfer, Paul, chaplain, born Oct. 2, 1915, Nuremberg, single. Ottoplatz 1.

Laurer, Maria, née Jerusalem von Salsenegg, born Dec. 2, 1887, Vienna, widow. Weidendamm 23/III.

Reitz, Walter, clerk, born July 25, 1904, Würzburg, married. Jäck St. 6/I.

Scheurer, Rudolf Michael, commercial apprentice, born July 24, 1925, Bamberg, single. Kunigundendamm 55/o.

Schutz, Otto, clerk, born June 8, 1924, Bamberg, single. Bleichanger 36.

Schwerin, Hildegard, clerk, born Dec. 19, 1923, Bamberg, single. Generalsgasse 2/I.

Simon, Lorenz, Clerk, born Nov. 2, 1918, Bamberg, single. Juden St. 3/III.

Steiner, Wilhelm, merchant, born Sept. 9, 1892, Ochsenfurth/Main, married. Au St. 2/III.

Veth, Elly, née Ensminger, born Nov. 13, 1911, Zabrze-Nord, near Hindenburg/Upper Silesia, married. Weide 7/o.

Wiedmann, Andrej Camillo, assistant photographer, born Aug. 14, 1917, Rottach/Egern, single. Obere König St. 14/II.

Zenk, Hildegard, office worker, born Sept. 22, 1910, Bamberg, single. Mühlwörth 12/I.

Above-listed First-Degree Mischlinge have German citizenship.

The once-large Jewish community of Bamberg had now shrunk to 12 people. Closer scrutiny of the list reveals that everyone it mentions lived in a so-called "privileged mixed marriage."

And this was the last chapter in the history of the Jewish community of Bamberg, long established and well known throughout the nineteenth and early twentieth centuries. No

longer does Bamberg count families with a worldwide reputa-
tion among its Jewish residents. This outcome was the realization of a prophecy by a German nationalist hate-monger, the
evangelical pastor F.B, who on October 23, 1923 published it in
a pamphlet entitled the *Coburg Warte* ("Coburg Watchtower"),
an organ of the Jungdeutscher Orden (abbrev. Jungdo).

ROMANIAN SUGGESTIONS ON THE SOLUTION OF THE JEWISH PROBLEM

A new pamphlet titled *Desteptarea Crestinismului* ("Awaken-
ing Christianity") has been published under the guidance of
Superior Stanic in Romania. It recommended the following
solution to the Jewish Question:

1. It is absolutely necessary to kill all Jews and to baptize all
   Moslems; otherwise the aspirations of Christianity are of
   no avail.
2. It is absolutely necessary to change the laws concerning
   name changes, so that nobody can remove himself from his
   nationality.
3. It is absolutely necessary to rescind the laws concerning
   Jewish emancipation.
4. It is absolutely necessary to burn down synagogues and
   Jewish schools; and what is left after the fire must be covered with earth, so that not a single stone will be visible.
5. It is absolutely necessary to confiscate all Jewish prayer
   books and Talmud volumes; they are the source of their
   curses and lies.
6. It is absolutely necessary to prevent the education of all
   Jews, whether public or private. They shall live in eternal
   slavery.

The course of history shows that the above "suggestions,"
published by someone who later became the bishop of his
church in Brunswick, were followed to the last letter.

NOTES
(Chapters 3–7)

Joseph Walk recently compiled a compendium of laws affect-ing Jews in the Third Reich, *Special Justice for Jews in the Nazi State: A Collection of Ordinances and Regulations, Their Contents and Their Import* (Karlsruhe, 1981).

The card file of the Registrar's Office is in the Bamberg Municipal Archives.

Events in Forchheim are recorded in the files of the Forch-heim County Seat. StAB K 9 XV #995.

Quotation by Walter Buch, *Deutsche Justiz* 100 (1936): 1660. The Führer's suggestion is in *Mein Kampf* (1940), p. 727; also mentioned by Domarus, *Speeches by Adolf Hitler*, January 30, 1939. Hans Günther Adler has done an in-depth study of the influence and effect of the bureaucracy on the Final Solution in *Der verwaltete Mensch* [The Organization Man]*: Studies of the Deportation of Jews from Germany* (Tübingen, 1974).

The imminent confiscation of the White Dove: StAB K 5 #3148. Bulletins of the Jewish community of Bamberg, which were the source of a great many portrayals of events, can be found in the Bamberg Municipal Archives, BS 473; also see Adler, p. 634, re: Surrender of jewelry and precious metals.

Functions and structures of Jewish organizations, see Adler, p. 354. Curfew at the beginning of the war, see Paul Sauer, *Documents Regarding the Persecution of Jewish Citizens in Baden-Württemberg by the Nazi Regime, 1933–1945*, Publications of the Baden-Württemberg State Archives, vol. 16 (Stuttgart, 1966); here, among many other references, was the accusation that Jews molested Aryan women during the blackout.

Marlis G. Steiner describes the mood at the beginning of the war in *Hitler's War and the German People: Mood and Attitude of* the German Population during World War II (Düsseldorf and Vienna, 1970).

There are many references to the less-than-heroic mood among the greater part of the population in the following diaries and memoirs: Lisa de Boor, *Pages from a Diary, 1938–1945* (Munich, 1963), p. 37; Jochen Klepper, *Under the Shadow of Your Wings: From Diaries of the Years 1938–1942* (Munich, 1964) (DTV #235–237), p. 253; Erich Ebermayer: . . . *and Tomorrow the Entire World: Memoirs of Germany's Dark Age* (Bayreuth, 1966), p. 424.

Maria Zelzer describes the confiscation of radio sets in Stuttgart on Yom Kippur in *Passage and Fate of the Jews in Stuttgart*, a commemorative book published by the city of Stuttgart, p. 213.

There is conflicting testimony about Karl Bezold; some describe him as a boisterous loudmouth, and others, among them some Jews, think of him as conciliatory.

Jewish medical attendants are covered in a file of the Health Department's district office, StAB M 30 #1046. The same file contains the notice of cessation of insulin treatment for Jews. Oral testimony given to the author by Dr. Georg Hornung (Bamberg) describes his encounter with Dr. Bauchwitz. Quotations about milk for Jewish children are from BA/R 58-169, Steinert, p. 247; confidential information 22/42 about food rations for Jews is from StAB M 30, #1046.

On deportations of Jews from Franconia, see Adler, p. 125, and Werner Schultheis, *Jews in Mainfranken, 1933–1945, with Special Reference to the Jews of Würzburg*, Contributions of Bad Neustadt to the General and Local History of Franconia, vol. 1 (Neustadt/Saale, 1980), a comprehensive work but difficult to follow; structure and typography make for tedious reading.

Adler, p. 125, describes the deportation from Vienna to Nisko; also the deportation of the Jews of Stettin. Letter to

Lammers is from IMT, NG 2490; on deportations of Jews from Baden and the Palatinate, see Sauer, vol. 2, p. 232.

On the National Railroad's involvement in the Final Solution, see Raoul Hilberg, *Special Trains to Auschwitz* (Darmstadt, 1978); the same author on the Final Solution in general in *The Destruction of European Jewry: A Complete History of the Holocaust* (Berlin, 1982).

On Riga and the Jungfernhof, see Gertrude Schneider, *Journey into Terror: The Story of the Riga Ghetto* (New York). Report of the Security Police in Libau: BA R 70 SU/20, p, 111. Documents about the prevention of emigration after November 1, 1941 can be found in the Bamberg Municipal Archives, s.v. "Jewish Emigrants." The notification from the Union of Jewish Communities is quoted by Sauer in vol. 2, p. 465.

List of deportees from Forchheim: StAB K 9 XV #995. Memo to assigned officers in Frankfurt: *Documentation of the History of the Jews of Frankfurt, 1933–1945* (Frankfurt/Main, 1963), p. 524.

Reports on the Nuremberg/Langwasser collection camp will be found in Arnd Müller, *History of the Jews of Nuremberg*.

Disclosures of conditions in the camps at Jungfernhof and Salaspils are from the transcript of the jury trial at Hamburg (50) 14/51 14 Js 210/49 in the case against the camp commandant of Jungfernhof (IFZ Gh 02. 05). Letter of Lange to Hinrich Lohse: Schneider, p. 128. Events in the Bikiernski Woods, Easter 1942, see Helmut Krausnik: *The Unit That Fought the War for the Weltanschauung* (Stuttgart).

The second deportation is described by Adler, p. 193, and also by Schulthess, p. 563. Signs of life from Izbica, see Adler, p. 468 and also the files of LRA BA in StAB.

Descriptions of deportations from Bamberg are, in one case, from interviews held by the Municipal Archives with former domestic help of Jewish families; in all other cases, from interviews conducted by the author.

A Theresienstadt "purchase contract" is in private hands in the United States (a photocopy is in the possession of the author). The reference to (uniformly administered nationwide) special account W is from Adler, p. 563. Letter from Karl Bezold: Bamberg Municipal Archives, BS 473. List of appraisals of pictures confiscated from Jewish owners: Yad Vashem, Jerusalem.

Article from the organ of the Jungdo: StAB K 3 Pr. reg.

Abbreviations

BA Federal Archives, Koblenz
IFZ Institute of Contemporary History, Munich
IMT International Military Tribunal
LRA Office of the County Seat
StAB Bamberg Municipal Archives

Appendix 1

The Jewish Community of Bamberg
1930–1938

SINCE THE OFFICIAL RECORDS of most German Jewish communities were destroyed or lost during the Holocaust years, their histories have to be reconstructed from the documents of the "other side." In the case of Bamberg, however, the situation is rather different. A large portion of the papers of the city's Jewish communal apparatus were confiscated after the Kristallnacht pogrom and deposited in the Bamberg Municipal Archive. The collection survived the war and subsequently ended up in the Central Archives for the History of the Jewish People in Jerusalem. Among these documents is a chronicle by Dr. Martin Morgenroth, president of the Bamberg Jewish community, recording communal activities from 1930, three years before Hitler came to power, up to the eve of Kristallnacht in 1938. With added poignancy and force because of its unadorned, objective style, the chronicle provides a unique glimpse at the daily life of Bamberg Jewry as it grappled with the ever-increasing repression imposed upon it by the Nazi regime.

1930

Dec. 21. Children's Hanukkah party at the *Ressource* [social club] with close to 1000 people present. A splendid celebration.

189

"Hanukkah in the Toy Shop," a well-performed skit, met with enormous applause. The recitation of Psalm 118 by the members of the youth group, arranged by Dr. Katten, left a deep impression on the audience.

Dec. 9. Mr. Maier Frank lost his life in an automobile accident at age 31.

Dec. 14. Mrs. Babette Treumann, wife of the highly respected president of the Central Verein,[1] Mr. Jakob Treumann, of blessed memory, died at the age of 76. Dr. Wassermann conveyed the sympathy of the C.V. in an eloquent eulogy. The departed was able to combine, to an outstanding degree, her love of country and commitment to faith.

Dec. 17. Miss Gitta Straus, 51, died after a long illness. A person with deep Jewish feelings. She worked for 25 years as the housekeeper of Mr. Hecht, of blessed memory.

Dec. 27. Mr. Joseph Bleicher, 62, died after a fulfilling life. He was a modest and unpretentious man.

The results of the yearly review of the congregation for the year 1930 show the death of 20 people and the birth of 7.

Dec. 28. First meeting of the new committees of the community. By mutual agreement an electoral contest was avoided. The administration added one seat to increase its membership to 10. After nearly 40 years as chairman, Privy Councilor Dr. Werner left Bamberg two months ago. The administration is now headed by Dr. Morgenroth, Esq.

Governing Bodies, Their Members and Jurisdictions

---

1 The Centralverein der Deutschen Juden (C.V.) was founded in the 1890s as a Jewish self-defense organization in response to rising anti-Semitism. (Ed.)

Administration: Dr. Morgenroth, chairman; J. Wassermann, vice-chairman and president of the synagogue; Dir. A. Weil, treasurer; F. Löble, corresponding secretary; J. Herrmann, administrator of endowments and vice-president of the synagogue; Also: Counselor J. Buxbaum, Engineer E. Heimann, Factory Owners M. Rossheimer and J. Schütz, Attorney Dr. S. Weichselbaum.

Executive Committee: chairman: Counselor W. Lessing; trustees: S. Ehmann, S. Brandes, Mrs. E. Fleissig, M. Goldschmidt, F. Grausmann, David Grunebaum, Leopold Gunzenhäuser, Counselor M. Höflein, R. Kalischak, Mrs. Anna Katz, Abr. Kohn, Is. Mayer, Anna Morgenroth, Justus Saalheimer, F. Silbermann, Dir. S. Simon, L. Schmitt, E. Stein, F. Stein, A. Sternglanz, M. Stoll, J. Strauss, W. Wachtel.

Committees and Their Members
1. Finance Committee: Silbermann, W. Lessing, Wachtel, Höflein, Ehmann, Fritz Stein.
2. Welfare Committee: Rossheimer, J. Herrmann, Heimann, Weil, Simon, Mayer, Grünebaum, Lessing, Strauss, Schmitt, Katz, Stoll.
3. Ritual and Worship Committee: Herrmann, Weichselbaum, Brandes, Saalheimer, Strauss.
4. Education Committee: Herrmann, Löbl, Weichselbaum, Simon, Goldschmidt, Brandes, Gunzenhäuser, Else Fleissig, Anna Katz.
5. Synagogue Choir Committee: Herrmann, Kohn, Krausmann;
Alternates: Mrs. Irma Kohn, Mrs. Berta Simon.

Dec. 27. The birth of a daughter, Eva Ellen, to Mr. Sigmund Buxbaum and his wife Mathilde, née Nauburger.

1931

Jan. 3. Mr. Eugen Rosenfeld, 68, died of encephalitis. Scion of an established Bamberg family, one of which was Rabbi Samson Wolf Rosenfeld, of blessed memory. Interment Jan 5.

Jan 5. Lecture by Dr. Katten at the Society for Jewish History and Literature. Topic: "How Did Our Sages Interpret the Bible?"

Jan. 6. Meeting of the executive committee. The motion to fill the position of burial attendant, formerly held by Mr. Samuel Brief, is rejected. The duties of the attendant will be assumed by the beadle.

Jan. 15. Mrs. Lina Löw, née Herrmann, 71, died of a stroke. Modest and devout, she attended the synagogue regularly.

Jan. 19. Burial of Jakob Fraenkel of Rottingen near Ochsenfurt, the brother of our former teacher, Fraenkel.

Jan. 30. Mr. Herrmann Walter, 76, died of a stroke.

Feb. 1. Dinner Meeting of the Chevra Kaddisha (Burial Society).

Feb. 12. Miss Marianne Hellmann passed away and was buried on the 13th. At the invitation of the rabbinate, several schools visited our synagogue. The students followed the explanations with great interest. They were visibly moved by the musical renditions of the synagogue choir. The reason for these presentations is to counteract the erroneous depictions of Jewish worship which are fed by the anti-Semitism of these troubled times. Apparently it helped us to reach some of our objectives. Participating schools in this project were the Humanistic Gymnasium, the Old Gymnasium, and the upper forms of the Real Gymnasium.

Feb. 13 and 14. The brothers Max and Josef Kupfer died. The former, after an operation in Erlangen; the latter of a heart attack, after receiving the news of his brother's death. A joint burial will take place on Feb. 17.

Feb. 23. Lecture by Prof. Unna, Nuremberg, at the Literary Society. Topic: "Bernard Shaw and the Jews."

Feb. 22. Leopold Gunzenhäuser, cattle dealer, died at the age of 61. A devout Jew, generous and modest. He was a member of the executive committee.

March 15. Lecture by Rabbi Emeritus Dr. Eckstein at the Literary Society. Topic: "Thoughts About the Religion of the Future and the Future of Religion."

Mar. 22. Miss Luise Hess died at the age of 52.

Apr. 11. The widow Minna Löwi, née Gutmann, died at the age of 74. A courageous, devout woman, who suffered through much grief.

Apr. 13. General Meeting of the C.V. and talk by Dr. Katten. Topic: "The New Apologetic Literature."

Apr. 2. For the first time, a community Seder was held in Bamberg. Dr. Katten conducted the Seder for 57 participants. All left the celebration with a sense of elation.

Apr. 23. Ludwig Haas, merchant, died at the age of 26 years and one month. Burial took place at his birthplace.

May 16. Privy Councilor Teitel, executive of the Union of Russian Jews, arrived in Bamberg to canvass members for his organization. A local branch was established.

May. The Teachers Conference, now in its second year, has proved its worth. Held every four weeks, the conference is directed toward the teachers of the district and offers them advanced training. Each conference is devoted to a specific topic, and by the end of the cycle each of the following Jewish subjects is addressed: History, Bible, Midrash, Instruction, Ethics, and Halacha (Law).

June 9. Counselor Max Guttmann died. Burial will be on the 10th.

Aug. 27. Wedding of Medical Doctor Alfred Kandel to Miss Maja Wachtel, daughter of Mr. Max Wachtel, both local residents.

Oct. 5. Widow Babette Dessauer, 81, died. According to her wishes, she was cremated.

Oct. 29. Died: Miss Fanny Oster, age 73 1/2.

Oct. 30. Birth of a son to Attorney Siegbert Weichselbaum and his wife Mosella, née Plaut.

Nov. 7. Mrs. Anna Baum, née Bettmann, died at the old-age home in Würzburg. She was the chairwoman of the women's Chevra in Bamberg. Burial on the 10th in Bamberg.

Nov. 22. Rabbi Bärwald of Munich gave a public lecture in our synagogue, the topic: "Job, the Book of Human Suffering." The presentation was received with great acclaim. The press gave rave reviews to the content and delivery of the speech.

Nov. 30. At the Society for Jewish History and Literature, Dr. Katten gave the first of a six-part lecture series, devoted to the topic: "Portraits from Jewish History." The extent of the interest in these lectures was evident from the size of the audience.

Dec. 6. The children's Hanukkah party took place in the big hall of the Ressource. On the program: recitations, musical numbers by the Nebel Band, a skit by the juniors of the Youth Organization, and a play by the smaller children: "A Mother's Dream."

Dec. 17. Mrs. Hedwig Oppenheimer, wife of the retired teacher, died at the age of 72. Diligent and generous.

Dec. 24. Died: Mrs. Marie Baum, née Kraus, 76. Modest and generous.

Population Statistics at the End of 1931
Previous total: 875; deaths: 15; births: 1; departures: 5; arrivals: 6. New total: 862.

1932
Jan 7. Lecture by Prof. Dr. Guttmann of Breslau at the Society for Jewish History and Literature. Topic: "The Human Aspect in the Old Hebrew Scriptures." The informative discourse was received with great applause.

Jan. 10. Mr. Moritz Kronacher, 74, died of arteriosclerosis, which caused a fall in the street. Diligent and kind.

Jan. 24. General meeting of the Chevra Kaddisha. Reelection of the board of trustees: Mr. Julius Wassermann, Dir. Albert Weil, and Mr. J. Herrmann. Mr. Wassermann read the constitution of the Chevra, dated 1772, according to which the society is over 210 years old. A resolution was adopted to convene the yearly meetings on the 7th of Adar, the anniversary of the death of Our Teacher Moses, or as close as possible to this date. Two 40-year members and a 25-year member received the thanks of the entire membership.

Jan. 25. H. Saki, merchant, moved to the parental home of his wife in Mühlhausen, Upper Franconia. Under the guidance of Referendar [Law Clerk) W. Aron, a German-Jewish youth group was organized. A successful party took place on Friday night. The establishment of this group drew opposition and caused friction, previously not felt. It is imperative to stay clear of rivalry and conflict based on differences of opinion and restrict the dispute to practical matters.

Jan 30. Mrs. Babette Sternberg, 83, died after a long illness. A person full of strength and fond of life.

Feb. 11. Miss Ellen Wassermann, daughter of Counselor Albert Wassermann, married Ernst Schöndorff in Berlin.

Feb. 9. Birth of a son, Ralph, to Josef Katz and his wife Martha, née Wiesenfelder.

Feb. 14. Lecture by Dr. Galliner at the Society for Jewish History and Literature. Topic: "Lesser Ury and His Artistic Milieu." The lively presentation was accompanied by excellent slides. The projection of pictures of Ury's work resulted in a clearer understanding of his creativity and at the same time defined his style of contemporary concepts and forms.

March 14. Lecture by Rabbi Emeritus Dr. Eckstein. Topic: "History of the Jews in Bamberg." The lecture's comprehensive approach, enhanced by many slides, drew great applause.

March 27. Mr. Max Morgenroth, 58, died after a long illness. A man of exceptional kindness, a generous philanthropist.

March 28. Mrs. Elsa Heinemann, age 83, died after a quiet, retiring life.

March 13. Get-together of the members of the C.V. on the evening of the national presidential elections. Comments by

C.V. Director Holländer aroused a palpable tension. Thanks to his extensive knowledge of national politics, he was able to explain the lasting impact of this event. Many remained to listen to the radio broadcast of the election results.

Apr. 4. Widow Hanne Reus died at the age of 68.

May 1. Departures: Mrs. Emma Hellmann, family J. Katz (4), fam. M. Rogozinsky (5) Leon Baum. A total of 11 people.

May 15. Mr. Hirsch (Hermann) Naumann, 63, passed away. He was devout and rigorously steadfast in his belief. He was the cantor of alternative Congregation Adass Yisroel for 22 years.[2]

June 1. Died: Mr. Sally Kalischak, 76, a quiet and retiring man.

June 10. Rabbi Emeritus Dr. Eckstein celebrated his 75th birthday. He was the recipient of many honors. The sermon on the first day of Shavuot [Feast of Weeks), coinciding with his birthday, acclaimed the merits of his works and the excellence of his teachings.

June 12. Mr. Samuel Brief, long-time caretaker at our cemetery, left Bamberg to live at the old-age home in Würzburg.

The spread of poverty, also affecting the Jewish population, was cause for some consideration: How to direct rootless German Jews to gainful employment, even work entailing physical exertion. The Federation of Jewish War Veterans is experimenting with training young Jews for agricultural work. Other organizations have followed in this direction. The Zionist

---

2 This Orthodox body was a private synagogue association outside the unified Gemeinde. In 1873 German law authorized the existence of such associations and permitted individuals to voluntarily withdraw from the official community in order to join them. (Ed.)

Organization was able to place four young men with farmers in the Bamberg vicinity. They will be trained as farmers and gardeners. Other Jewish organizations are trying similar experiments. Steps taken by Agudath Israel met with difficulties, due to the need to fulfill certain religious requirements. The rabbi's office has circulated an appeal regarding this matter.

June 1. Arrival: Superior Justice Kahn, a new member. (Wife and children are gentile). (+1)

July 1. Arrival: Josef Spier and family. (+3)

Aug. 21. Wedding of Miss Margot Herrmann, daughter of Mr. Julius Herrmann, Bamberg, to Attorney Dr. Karl Bier, Frankfurt. Hechalutz [the Jewish Pioneers) with the help of the local branch of the Zionist Organization has been able to place six young people (including three girls) as apprentices with farmers and gardeners. These young people have established their own home at Steinweg 15. They were assisted by the munificence of our local Jewish citizens. This venture is the first of its kind in Bavaria and may entail a certain risk in these difficult times.

Aug. 3. Mr. Neumann Frank celebrated his 90th birthday in excellent mental health.

Sept. 1. Herman H., merchant, 72, died as the result of a self-inflicted bullet-wound.

Sept. 3. Mrs. Basalie Feldheim, née Rödelheimer, 75, died after a prolonged illness.

Aug. 15. Samuel Rosenfelder, merchant, moved to Nuremberg.

(Population decrease of 1 person.)

Aug. 28. Wedding in Berlin of Miss Selma Hirnheimer, daughter of Mr. Max Hirnheimer, Bamberg.

Sept. 1. Due to marital difficulties, Mr. Rudolf Fleischmann resigned his job and left Bamberg with his oldest son. (-2)

Sept. 15. Leopold Kaufmann, retired, Franz-Ludwig St. 11, moved to Frankfurt/Main. (-2)

Sept. 15. It will be of great interest to coming generations to be able to consult a statistical profile of the Jewish community of Bamberg. The following numbers clearly show an abnormal trend. They reveal the situation today and also signal the slow demise and withering of German Jewry. By following the descending curve it is possible to pinpoint with mathematical certainty the cessation of a Jewish community in Bamberg. A preponderance of older people is evident. Most married people have few children or none. Younger people find it extremely difficult to establish themselves in self-supporting occupations. Deprived of an economic basis, accompanied by a dearth of jobs, they are reluctant to establish families. Even those in secure positions show an aversion to marriage. The reason may lie in the fear of being saddled with the obligation of supporting parents and relatives.

The following survey dates to Sept. 15, 1932:
287 households, including 186 headed by married couples.
182 with Jewish partners, 4 mixed marriages (the wife being the gentile partner). Six mixed marriages, where the husband is the Christian partner, are not included in this survey. Out of 186 marriages, 31 are without children; only 12 have more than 3 children. The rest of the population consists of 13 widowers and 83 widows; 39 are older bachelors and 27 are women past reproductive age.

110 people are between the ages of 20 and 30 (the most likely time for marriage), 57 male and 53 female.

88 are of school age (extended to the age of 19 on the assumption that most will have continued into higher education).

47 are boys and 41 girls.

44 are preschool children: 21 boys and 23 girls.

152 are 60 years old or above. This is the break-down:

Age 60–70: 81,40 male,41 female

70–80: 57,27 male,30 female

80–90: 11, 3 male, 8 female

There are 2 males and 1 female over the age of 90.

Sept. 21. Mrs. Adele Lessing, née Obermeyer, 81, died after a long illness. She had strength of mind and strong family ties. Burial on Sept. 23.

Sept. 30. Miss Marie Gütermann, 67, died after a prolonged illness. Vivacious and good-natured. Burial on Oct. 2, the second day of Rosh Hashanah.

Addendum

Apr. 1. Mr. Salo Dorn and family moved to Mannheim. (-3)

Sept. 15. Arrival: Mr. and Mrs. Selmar Bütow (Lending Library). (+2)

Oct. 2. On the second day of Rosh Hashanah, the 85th birthday of the President of the Reich [Hindenburg) was commemorated. During the Prayer for the Government and the Fatherland at the synagogue services, Rabbi Katten praised the 85-year old President as the true representative of the Fatherland.

Oct. 3. The new building for ritual slaughter of fowl was dedicated. The old location in an exposed lot did not conform to the requirements of hygiene and cleanliness. Slaughters performed in the open attracted an unwelcome audience. This necessitated the erection of an enclosed and functional building. It was built on the property of the old synagogue and has access by a private side street. The current owner of the property, St. Otto Publishers, assured the congregation of the right to rent the site for a number of years. The old location at Generalsgasse 15 was given to the firm of St. Otto as security. The cost of the building was approximately 2,500 rm.

Oct. 6. Birth of a son to Eng. Ludwig Schmitt and his wife Sitta, née Bein.

Sept. 10 (Addendum). Arrival: Rolf Hattensleben, merchant, from Munich. Residence: Schönleinsplatz 2. (+1)

Sept. 15. Arrival: Albert Schlossheimer, merchant, from Nuremberg, Sophienstr. 9. (+1)

Sept. 12. Arrival: Ernst Wasserstrom, manager, from Nuremberg, Nonnenbrücke 7. (+1)

Sept. 15. Arrival: Emil Wolff, merchant, from Würzburg, Kapuziner St. 31. (+2)

Sept. 15. Departure: Mrs. Bertha Erlanger, Mr. Siegfried Kronacher.

Oct. 22. Joseph S., 24, only son of Widow Therese S., died by his own hand.

Oct. 22. Return of Mr. Ludwig Fleischmann, Mr. Hermann Sacki.

"During services on Saturday the Jewish community of Bamberg remembered their sons who gave their lives in the World War. Rabbi Katten eulogized these heroes who died for the Fatherland at the side of their brothers of different faiths. The publication of a Memorial Book to the 12,000 Jewish service-men who gave their lives, bears witness to the sacrifices of the Jewish community. Prof. Hild led the synagogue choir in a moving recital, complementing the service. A large audience participated with exalted spirit in this solemn service" (*Bamberger Volksblatt*, Nov. 14, 1932).

Nov. 1. Arrival: Mr. Max Reichmann, Hain St. 12.

Nov. 20. Mass appeal for Keren Hayessod. The speakers were Dr. Oscar Wassermann, member of our congregation, and Dr. Traub. They addressed an overflow audience at the Ressource Hall on the topic: "The Condition of German Jewry Today." Dir. Wassermann described the disintegration of world Jewry. National politics of host countries, relaxation of strict religious practices, language barriers in all parts of the Old and the New World endanger the unity of Judaism. Palestine will be the unifying symbol for world Jewry. Dr. Traub pointed to the decline of Judaism in Eastern Europe. This alone will justify full support for a program to rebuild Palestine, he commented.

Nov. 27. The community held a prayer meeting in the synagogue. It attracted a wide audience. Donations of 159 marks benefited the Winter Relief program of Bamberg. The meeting started with the song *U'venuchu Yomar* followed by "The Day of the Lord" from the Kol Nidre liturgy. The sermon of Rabbi Katten, "The God of Love in the Old Testament," was the high point of the meeting. The festivities concluded with two songs performed by the choir: *Socharti lach* to the melody of the Rosh Hashanah service and "Praise the Lord," a moving German hymn.

Dec. 7. Rabbi Eschenbacher, Düsseldorf, lectured at the Society for History and Literature. His interesting topic: "Judaism, the State and Humanity." His speech culminated in this sentence: "Only those who draw on their inner resources, only Jews with self-confidence can offer their best to the nation."

Dec. 5. Birth of a son (Kurt Leo—Yehuda bar Micha) to Max Sacki, merchant, and his wife Lily, née Gutmann.

Dec. 20. Died: Salomon Lipp, merchant, 70. He was esteemed for his diligence and honesty. He opened a center for Jewish youth in his house on Amalien St. 10, to meet the need for accommodations allowing young people to gather for discussions and cultural activities. This rented space met those purposes. A large room is used as a lecture hall. Two smaller rooms can be used for study and recreation. The Bamberg Volksbildungsverein is the lease-holder and holds the rights to the premises. The rent is paid by the congregation, which has a free hand in its use. The relocation of the community's library and reading room there is in the planning stage.

Dec. 21. Died: Mrs. Lotte Klein, 83, an honorable and diligent woman.

Dec. 31. Died: Mrs. Fritzi Marx, née Schwarzmann, 79. A diligent woman and devoted mother.

Population Statistics, End of 1932
End of 1931—862 persons.
Decrease: Deaths—16, departures—24, out-of-town marriages—3.
Increase: Births—3, Arrivals—12.
End of 1932—834 persons.

1933
Jan. 12. Dedication of the new Youth Center at Amalien St. 10. Speeches by the president of the community, the rabbi, and representatives of participating organizations.

Jan. 15. 10th anniversary of the local branch of the Zionist organization, celebrated with a party at Harmony Hall.

Jan. 16. Lecture by Dr. Gundesheimer, Frankfurt/Main at the Society for Jewish History and Literature. Topic: "The Jews in Ancient Rome." Slides provided a good insight into Jewish art in Rome up to the year 250 A.D. Motifs in stone, glass, and print were shown to have a marked Jewish influence.

Jan. 18. Lecture by Dr. S. Auerbach, Würzburg, at the Jewish Youth Center. Topic: "Jewish Teachings." The approach was from an Orthodox viewpoint.

Jan. 15. Moved to Nuremberg: Max Rosenfelder family. (-2)

Jan. 15. Arrival: Attorney Dr. Stephen Fried. (+1)

Jan. 24. Died: Widow Regina Neuburger, 88. (-1)

Feb. 6. Lecture by Dr. Meyer, Nuremberg, at the Society for Jewish History and Literature. Topic: "The Private Spinoza."

Feb. 19. Party by the Jewish youth group. Proceeds to go to the C.W.K. This successful party was well attended. Many visitors came from out of town. The band, made up of local talent, was a great hit. The humor of emcee Fritz Stein captivated the audience.

Feb. 20. Rabbi Emeritus Dr. Eckstein published a record of local history. The congregation arranged for the printing, and proceeds were earmarked for the winter-relief fund. The title: *The Jewish Community in Bamberg: Pictures of the Past.*

Feb. 20. Departures: Mrs. Engelmann (-1); emigrated to Palestine: Mr. Erich Mannheim. (-1)

Feb. 28. Miss Bertha Blumenrath moved to Essen, Friedberg St. 49. (-1)

Mar. 2. Mrs. M.A. committed suicide. Burial Mar. 5.

Mar. 6. Babette Fleischmann of Aufsess, the oldest Jewish woman in the Bamberg district, died 9 days before her 100th birthday. Burial on March 8. Eulogy by Dr. Katten.

Mar. 5. Arrival: Mr. Dorn, Erlangen. (+1)

Mar. 24. Wedding of Mr. Egon Krieger, son of Mr. Heinrich Krieger, Bamberg, and Miss Sara Wolkenfeld, Nuremberg. The couple will depart in the coming days and settle in Palestine. (-1)

March 15. In the wake of the take-over by the new regime, the following members of our community were arrested on suspicion of subversive activities: Attorney W. Aron, Mr. Rimple, manager of the Tietz Department Store, and Mrs. Fraustädter.

Mar. 28. Mr. Siegfried Frank died after long suffering. (-1)

Mar. 28. A sign of the times. Quotation from the *Bamberger Volksblatt:* "Are we to expect hostile action against the Jews? The decision lies with the high command of the Nazi Party."

Apr. 2. Engagement of Mr. Max Wetzlar to Miss Frida Thiele, who converted to Judaism. (+1)

Apr. 5. Mr. Rudi Wallenstein, bank clerk, settled in Palestine. (-1)

Apr. 16. Burial in Bamberg of Mrs. Bertha Grünebaum, widow of our teacher. She resided here until 1931.

Due to new regulations, two lawyers from our congregation lost their licenses to practice. They are Mr. Weichselbaum and

Mr. Stephan Fried. The law restricts the right to practice of non-Aryan lawyers to the following categories: established prior to 1914, service at the front during the World War, or loss of father or son in the war.

All those in protective custody were released, except Attorney W. Aron. Calm prevailed during the boycott of Jewish businesses on March 31. Most establishments closed voluntarily. The branch of the Heimann shoe store, allegedly under Czech ownership, was closed by the police because of alleged exchange violations.

Arrival: Mr. and Mrs. Gustav Strauss, Munich. Hain Str 28. (+2)

Departure: Mr. Erwin Veith, actor, to Haifa.

May 1. As of today all ritual slaughter in the German Reich is prohibited. There is hope that imports of kosher meat from abroad will be permitted. The law covers all animals, including fowl. Consequently the building for ritual slaughter of fowl was sealed. By sheer luck, our two butcher shops had some reserves of kosher meat. Hopefully, they will last for a few weeks, perhaps three months. Members of the congregation are advised to keep consumption to a minimum.

May 3. Mrs. Jeanette Ordenstein died shortly after her 89th birthday. Mrs. Ordenstein was the daughter of Dr. Dessauer, former president of our community. She succumbed to burns sustained while lighting a gas stove. According to her wishes she was cremated.

Second Teacher Conference. Lecture by Schapiro. Topic: "Feuchtwanger's Novel *The Jewish War* and Its Historical Background." The first conference in 1933 took place at the end of March. The speaker was Bauda, Demmelsdorf. Topic: "The Use of Rashi's Commentaries in the Teaching of Jewish Scriptures."

Arrival: Mr. Oppenheimer and family. (+3)

May 9. Merchant Adolf Himmelreich, 65, died after an intestinal operation. (-1)

May 15. Miss Trude Krieger, daugher of Abraham Krieger, tailor, left Bamberg to settle in Palestine. (-1)

May 15. Mrs. Toni Laufer, 60, died suddenly. Her granddaughter Ilse Rosenbaum will move to her aunt in Saarlouis. (-2)

May 15. Attorney Wilhelm Aron died suddenly at the Dachau concentration camp near Munich at the age of 27. He and five other Jewish prisoners had been transferred there from Hofheim. The official death certificate listed pneumonia as the cause of death. By order of the criminal police, the coffin, sealed in Dachau, was not to be opened. The return of their talented and idealistic only son under these circumstances was a hard blow to his parents.

May 22. Wedding of Franz Stern, M.D., Würzburg, and Miss Marianne Holzinger, daughter of Dr. Otto Holzinger, pharmacist, Bamberg. The couple will emigrate to England. The witnesses were J. Hessberg and Dr. Herzfelder.

May 20. Arrival: Gunzenhäuser family, Memmelsdorf, Lower Franconia. (+3)

May 22. Founded: Committee for Aid and Rehabilitation. Task: to aid in training and help in preparing for emigration; also the solicitation of funds for this project.

May 28. Attorney Dr. Siegfried Weichselbaum will leave Bamberg with his family to seek new fortunes in Palestine. Dr. Weichselbaum was an outstanding member of our administration. He was an advocate of every good cause. He counseled and supported many in their legal predicaments, often without compensation. His departure leaves a deep void. He was a mentor to the Zionist youth group, helping them in their personal and spiritual quests. (-5)

May 1. Max Reichmann and family moved to Berlin. (-2)

May 19. Mrs. Mannheim moved to her daughter in Liegnitz. (-1)

May 30. The Neumann Franks celebrated their 65th wedding anniversary in vigorous health and good spirits. Mr. and Mrs. Karl Kohn celebrated their golden anniversary.

June 8. Third Teachers Conference. Lecture by Erlebacher, Mühlhausen. Topic: "*The Desert and the Promised Land*, by Elias Auerbach." The early history of Israel stimulated a discussion on the history of ancient oriental civilizations.

June 14. Mr. Julius Wassermann celebrated his 60th birthday. He was a recipient of numerous tokens of esteem. The rabbi's office awarded him the title of *chaver* in honor of his service to the congregation, especially in behalf of charity. The honoree received an inscribed document.

June 12. The first shipment of kosher meat from Denmark was offered for sale, as the entire old stock in the butcher shops was exhausted. The high price of the meat (1.60 reichmarks per pound) will cause a great reduction in the consumption of meat. The congregation is worried about the ability of poorer families to afford meat. Unfortunately, many former consumers of kosher meat, without really pressing need, switched to *trefa* meat. Only 40 to 50 families will remain consumers of kosher meat.

June 15. Mrs. Jenny Rimpel, 57, wife of Nathan Rimpel, died after agonizing suffering. Burial will be in Kitzingen. (-1) To minimize the terrible effects of the recent political upheaval, an optional third hour of religious instruction has been instituted. A stronger awareness of Jewish values will act as a counterbalance to any feelings of inferiority. The response to these uplifting lectures has been very good. People past school age are encouraged to participate.

June 25. To replace Dr. Weichselbaum, Mr. Julius Strauss became a member of the administration. A resolution passed to lower the church tax for the year 1934 from 15% to 12%. A fund drive of the Committee for Aid and Rehabilitation is under way. In general there is an understanding of the need for these measures, and the time-honored Jewish support for charity will prevail.

July 5. Rudi Marx, son of Mr. Hugo Marx, moved to Palestine. (-1)
Arrival: L. Mosbacher and wife from Kronach. (+2)

July 15. Arrival: Mrs. Nanni Katten from Marburg. (+1)
Memorial to Theodor Herzl at the synagogue on the 29th anniversary of his death.

Sept. 9. Hans Goldmann and Berthold Cysner settled in Palestine. (-2)
The following girls emigrated abroad: Ilse Hessberg, Martha and Ilse Steinberg, Hilde Fleissig, Carola Felsenstein, a total of 5.

Oct. 1. Mrs. Lea Böttigheimer and daughter Liesel emigrated to Amsterdam. (-2) Jakob Liffmann moved to Düsseldorf, his daughter to America. (-2)

Oct. 25. Mrs. Amalie Sulzbacher, née Lust, died at the age of 92 1/2. She was the oldest woman in our congregation. (-1)

Oct. 15. Ludwig Schmitt, his wife, and his son Franz emigrated to Palestine. His replacement on the board of directors is Mr. Langguth. (-3)

Oct. 31. Speech by Rabbi B. Jacob, Augsburg, at the synagogue. Topic: "The Servant of God."

Nov. 3. At a meeting of the Jewish Youth Organization of Bamberg, it was decided to carry on with the regular activities. An interdict by the police in June 1933 caused the interruption. Regular gatherings for Jewish educational activities, entertainment, and recreation will resume. Overall guidance by Dr. Katten. Reading Circle: Luitpold Neumann. Recreation and Entertainment: Kleestadt. Secretary: H. Blum. Treasurer: Neumann. Deputy Leader: Schapiro.

Nov. 13. Mr. and Mrs. Simon Michels celebrated their golden wedding anniversary.

Nov. 15. Arrival: Mr. and Mrs. Adolf Marx from Bayreuth. (+2)

Dec. 1. Arrivals: Julius Schönthal family from Hofheim. (+4) Fein family from Hofheim. (+4)

Dec. 14. Hanukkah celebration of the Jewish youth group in the Little Synagogue, followed by a party.

Dec. 23. Mrs. Jenny Mondschein celebrated her 90th birthday.

Dec. 30. Heinrich Zarnowietzki emigrated to Palestine. (-1)

Population Statistics, End of 1933
End of 1932—834

Departures: Death—9
Relocation—8
Arrivals: Birth—0
Conversion—1
Total—821

1934

Jan. 1. Mrs. Anna Rödelheimer and daughter moved to Rattach. (-2)
Arrival: Mr. and Mrs. Heymann and family. (+4)

Jan. 4. Lecture by Julius Bab at the synagogue. Topic: "Goethe and the Jews."

Jan. 10. Died: Mr. Lazarus Himmelreich, 92, former grain and cattle dealer. (-1)

Jan. 18. Died: Ida F., widow of Karl Friedrich (suicide). (-1)

Jan. 28. Died: Max Heymann, merchant, 61. (-1)

Feb. 9. Died: Hermann Lehmann, 78, retired merchant. (-1)

Feb. 11. Mr. Leo Ansbacher, Schesslitz, appointed custodian of the synagogue. Increase of population +3.

Feb. 24. Died: Mrs. Amalie Charlotte Federlein, née Baum, at the age of 82. (-1)

Apr. 4. Alfred Katz family settled in Palestine. (-4)

Apr. 18. Ernst Cysner settled in Palestine. (-1)

Apr. 1. Mrs. Anne Rödelheimer returned. (+1)

May 16. Died: Simon Felsenstein, 73, lumber wholesaler. (-1)

June 3. Marriage of Miss Paula Hinsheimer to Mr. Arthur Meyer, Oberlauringen. (-1)

June 11. Marriage of Mrs. Änne Grünebaume (divorced wife of Mr. Fleischmann) to the widower Karl Selig, Nordhausen/Harz. Her son is Werner Fleischmann. (-2)

Aug. 5. Miss Gabriele Hessberg married Mr. Adolf Schwarzkopf, Zurich. (-1)

Aug. 5. Arrivals: Schloss family from Neustadt/Aisch (+4), Mr. Otto Rosenblüth. (+2)
Sept. 5. Died: Mr. Hermann Hess, 72. Cremation. (-1)
Five girls who left Sept. 9, 1933, returned. (+5)

Oct. 10. Died: Mr. Neumann Frank, 92, Bamberg. (-1)
Arrivals: Dingfelder family from Uhlfeld (+3), Erich Jacobson family (+3), Siegfried Liebau family (+2), Family Alfred Hess, (his wife is Christian). (+1)

Oct. 14. Burial of Mr. Max Wassermann, 72. He died in Berlin.
Wedding of Mr. Leo Meyer, Zerf/Mosel, and Miss Leni Wiesenfelder, daughter of Emanuel Wiesenfelder, local merchant. (-1)

Oct. 27. Sudden death of merchant Fritz Treumann, 50. (-1)
Miss Bertha Elter left Bamberg; after a short period of training in Holland, she settled in Palestine. (-1)

Oct. 29. Wedding of Martin Mannheimer, Coburg, and Miss Zensi Reichmannsdorfer, Trabelsdorf.
Concert by the violin virtuoso Stephan Frenkel at the synagogue, sponsored by the Kulturbund of Jewish Communities in Bavaria.

Nov. 4. Lecture by Ernst Simon. Topic: "Jeremiah and His Message for Our Times." His stirring speech left a lasting impression.

Nov. 20. Mrs. Hanni Elter left Bamberg. (-1)

Nov. 21. Mrs. Gertrud Kohn, née Dingfelder, wife of Mr. Karl Kohn, died on her 76th birthday. (-1)
Addendum: Arrival: Adler family. (+3)

Nov. 28. Died: Mrs. Malwine Herz, née Blumenthal, 81. (-1)

Dec. 4. Died: Felix Silbermann, merchant, 59. He was gentle and good-natured. (-1)

Dec. 7. Hanukkah festival at the synagogue, including the recitation of Hebrew songs and rounds, speeches by Dr. Terluz, director of Jewish youth groups in Bavaria; Fritz Stein, leader of the local branch and Dr. Morgenroth, president of the community. The high point was a sermon by the rabbi: "Hanukkah and Jewish Youth."

Dec. 9. An evening of readings by Mrs. Herrnstadt, Öttingen. Her masterful recitations turned the evening into a memorable experience.

Dec. 10. Died: Mrs. Jette Huth, née Nordschild. She resided with her sister.

Dec. 23. Marriage of Miss Alice Rossheimer to Mr. Edward Levinsohn, Weissenfeld/Thuringia. (-1)

Dec. 26. Died: Mrs. Sophie Ehmann, 56, wife of Mr. Berthold Ehmann. Good-natured and respected. (-1)
Arrival: Mrs. Strauss and two daughters from Munich. (+3)

Population Statistics, End of 1934

Population end of 1933—821
Decrease: Death—16
Marriage—6
Relocation—9
Total—790
Increase: Birth—0
Return—6
Arrival—26
Total—824

1935

Jan. 1. Arrival: Mrs. Schwed, mother-in-law of Mr. Jakob Fleischmann. (+1)
Anton Lessing family moved to Berlin. (-2)

Jan 12. Death of Rabbi Emeritus Dr. Adolf Eckstein at the age of 78. He was the rabbi and leader of our community for many years. He will be remembered for his unstinting work and his well-known academic lectures.

Jan 13. Funeral of Rabbi Eckstein at the Bamberg cemetery.
According to the wishes of the deceased, there was only a brief ceremony. At graveside he was eulogized by Rabbi Katten; Dr. Morgenroth, president of the community; Dr. Masur, of Coburg, as the representative of the affiliated congregations; Rabbi Emeritus Dr. Freudenthal, Nuremberg, as the representative of the many organizations Dr. Eckstein was connected with, and also as a personal friend. On the following Sabbath, at the conclusion of the evening prayers, a memorial service took place. Dr. Morgenroth had eloquent praise for the departed for his tireless devotion to the congregation. Rabbi Katten reviewed the eventful life of the deceased. The *Journal of*

the Jewish Congregations in Bavaria will publish a detailed obituary of Rabbi Adolf Eckstein, of blessed memory.

Jan. 20. Sermon by Rabbi Salzberger, Frankfurt. Topic: "The Fate and the Mission of the Synagogue in Judaism." Mr. Gerd Palm entertained with a violin recital before and after the speech.

Jan. 22. Benno Weiss emigrated to Palestine. (-1)

Feb. 2. Died: Mrs. Hannchen Bretzfelder, 72. Loyal and devout. (-1)

Feb. 10. Died: Mrs. Eva Wolf, née Bernet, 84, of a gastric disorder. (-1)
Mrs. Bettmann and her son Semi moved to Augsburg.(-2)
Dr. Lang and wife moved to Wiesbaden. (-2)
Heinrich Krieger and family moved to Palestine. (-3)

Feb. 28. Mr. Emil Massmann died in Salzburg while visiting his daughter. (-1)

Mar. 7. Birth: Michael, son of Herbert Lindner. (+1)

Mar. 10. Arrival: Mr. Hermann Fleischmann and daughter Sali (+2).

Mar. 15. Children's Purim party. Recitations and songs.

Mar. 30. The congregation held a memorial service in honor of the 800th birthday of Maimonides. Prof. Ismar Elbogen, Berlin, spoke eloquently about the Rambam's life and work. Song recitals before and after the speech by Miss Berta Oster and Cantor Lent.

Apr. 7. Wedding of Mr. Erich Katzenstein, clerk, and Miss Marianne Rödelheimer of Bamberg.

Apr. 9. Died: Mrs. Cäcilie Schubert, née Oppenheimer, 68. (-1)

Apr. 14. Wedding of Mr. Felix Hahn, son of Mr. Aron Hahn and Miss Anni Ullmann, daughter of the late Simon Ullmann, both of Bamberg.

Apr. 14. Concert by a trio of artists from Nuremberg, Mrs. Frank, Mrs. Soren, and Mr. Grünebaum, at the synagogue. The outstanding performance was greeted with well-deserved applause.

July 3. Died: Max Früh, merchant, 61. (-1)

July 15. Emanuel Merel fammily settled in Palestine. (-4)

Aug. 11. Wedding of Gerda Welt, daughter of Mr. Moritz Welt, Bamberg, and Mr. Hermann Marx, Frankfurt/Main. (-1)

Aug. 2. Birth of a daughter to Mr. Alfred Hess. (+1)

July 15. Mr. Ludwig Oppenheimer and family emigrated to America. (-3)

Sept. 15. Celebration of the 25th anniversary of our synagogue. Among the many celebrants were Justice of the High Court Dr. Neumeyer, Munich, and numerous visitors from out of town. The mood was solemn. The festivities began with an organ recital and the song *Ma Tovu*. A poem by Miss Hilde Marx and greetings by Justin Isner set the tone, reflecting the aura of these troubled times. Dr. Morgenroth, president of the congregation, emphasized in his speech the venerable age and time-honored traditions of our community. Handel's *Arioso*, sung by Mrs. Bertha Simon, and a violin solo added to the solemn mood. The speech by Dr. Katten pointed to the fickle fate of our times and remembered the men and women who made the construction of this synagogue possible. Justice Neumeyer conveyed the greetings of the Union of Jewish Communities of Bavaria and emphasized the importance and value of the Bamberg community to all the members of the Union. Cantor Lent's recital and the *Hallelujah Chorus* concluded the festivities. This was our last celebration as citizens of the German Reich.

Sept. 16. Died: Mr. Simon Marx, 81. (-1)
Arrival: Mrs. Fischel and children, Heinz and Lotte, from Bonn. (+3)

Sept. 18. Died: Miss Jeanette Neumann, 72. (-1)

Oct. 24. Recital by soloist Paula Lindberg. The program included songs by Handel, Schubert, and Mahler, which met with enthusiastic applause.

Oct. 27. Mr. Ludwig Goldmaier, Lichtenfels, married Miss Bella Bamberger, daughter of Adolf Bamberger of Bamberg. (+1)
Karl Wisenfelder and Fritz Ehrlich emigrated to Palestine. (-2)
Heinz and Paul Kahn emigrated to Argentina. (-2)
Kurt Mondschein emigrated to South Africa. His father relocated to a convalescent home in Würzburg. (-2)

Nov. 8. Readings by the author Dr. Artur Erloesser at the synagogue. Topic: "Joseph's Role in World Literature."

Nov. 20. Mr. Samuel Rosenfelder emigrated to Palestine. (-1)
Permission was given to reopen the Chalutz Home, which had been closed by order of the police. Private benefactors donated the furnishings.

Dec. 7. Died: The widow Bertha Felsenstein, née Mayer, after a long illness. (-1)

Dec. 8. Readings by Mrs. Herrnstadt, Öttingen. The famous artist again demonstrated her unique talents.

Dec. 11. The congregation acquired the property at Generalsgasse 10 and 12, the White Dove Inn. Jewish travelers, deprived of accommodations in Aryan hotels, will now be able to stop in a place with a welcoming atmosphere. There will be room to spare, so that other organizations, such as youth groups, educational institutes, etc., can be accommodated. The purchase price is 55,000 reichmarks. After structural modifications the building should be ready in six months.

Dec. 12. Died: The widow Paula Stein, 70, of heart failure. (-1)

Dec. 25. Hanukkah festival. Sermon by Rabbi Katten. Topic: "Four Times Joseph" (the biblical Joseph, Flavius Josephus, Don Joseph Nasi, and Micha Josef Berdyczewski). The speech was followed by Miss Hilda Marx's recitation of her own poems. Special invitations to all the congregations in the district attracted many out-of-town visitors.

Dec. 28. Mr. Ludwig Freudenthal emigrated to Argentina. (-1) Mrs. Schwer emigrated to Agram (i.e., Zagreb).

Population Statistics, End of 1935
Population at the end of 1934—824
Decrease: Death—10
Departures—27
Out-of-town marriage—1
Total—786
Increase: Birth—2
Arrival—5
Marriage—2
Total—795

1936

Jan 12. Samuel Brief, former longtime caretaker at our cemetery, died at the old-age home in Würzburg. Mrs. Ricke Goldbach, née Bruckmann, of Würzburg, was buried in Bamberg.

Jan. 13. Mr. Arnold Lehmann emigrated to Palestine. (-1)

Jan. 1. Mr. Erich Spier emigrated to Holland. (-1)
Arrival: Family Oppenheimer (mother and 3 sons). (+3)

Feb. 1. Dr. Michael Wassermann and family moved to Prague. (-4)

Feb. 13. Died: Mr. Rudolf Stein, 76. (-1)

Feb. 16. Wedding of Mr. Arnold Mayer and Miss Anni Levor, both of Bamberg. The couple will emigrate to America. (-2)

Feb. 22. Mrs. David Rothschild left Bamberg and will live with her children in the U.S.A. (-1)
Miss Margot Wassermann emigrated to South Africa. (-1)
Privy Councilor J. Werner retired from the board of directors of the Union of Jewish Communities of Bavaria. The president of our congregation, Dr. Morgenroth, took his place.

Feb. 25. Mr. Max Rosenfelder, formerly of Bamberg, died in Nuremberg. Burial took place in Bamberg.

Mar. 1. Annual meeting of the Chevra Kaddisha [Burial Society]. Mr. Julius Wassermann read the annual report. Several proposals to change the by-laws were submitted. Dr. Katten gave a lecture on the history of the Chevra Kaddisha in Germany.

Mar. 20. Died: Recha Palm, wife of Mr. Erich Palm. (-1)
Their son Gerd Palm emigrated to America. (-1)

Mar. 22. Mr. Manfred Fein emigrated to America. (-1)
Concert by the Munich Art Trio at the synagogue.

Mar. 29. Died: Mr. Theodore Bachmann, 67. (-1)

Apr. 1. Lecture by Dr. Willy Cohn, Bamberg, at the synagogue. Topic: "Jewish History: A Proud Past and an Important Responsibility in the Future." The lecture summarized Jewish history from a Zionist viewpoint and was highly instructive. Entertainment was provided by Mrs. Rosenfelder, Nuremberg, with a splendid recital of songs by Dvorak, Wolf, and Schubert.

Apr. 1. The community takes possession of the White Dove Inn. A few structural modifications and repairs remain to be completed. A partition will divide the kitchen for dairy and meat use. Mr. Schlossheimer will be in charge of beverages; Mrs. Mondschein, food. It is now up to the community to turn the restaurant into a going concern.

Apr. 2. Miss Lotte Fischel moved to Berlin to train as a nurse. (-1)
Arrival: Kurt, son of Mr. Rudolf Fleischmann from Mühlheim. (+1)
Died: Mr. Moritz Steinberger, 79. Devout Jew and kindhearted. (-1)

Apr. 7. Died: Mrs. Lina Jungerwirth, 75. (-1)

Apr. 11. Died: Joseph Obermeier, formerly of Bamberg, the owner of a brick factory, died in Gundelsdorf. He was cremated in Coburg.

Apr. 19. Miss Mathilde Fleischmann, Hofheim, died suddenly of a liver ailment. She was here to care for her sick brother, Rudolf. Burial will be in Kleinsteinach.

May 3. Died: Mrs. Dora Gerst, 79. (-1)

May 7. Dedication of the White Dove Inn took place this evening. Thirty people stayed for a festive dinner. All facilities are new. A wall divides the kitchen for dairy and meat use; both under the management of Mrs. Mondschein. The ambiance is conducive to a relaxed mood. A special feature is the magnificent garden. A brochure will be printed to acquaint a wider clientele with our establishment.

May 10. Mrs. Hannchen Neumann and her children, Luitpold and Lili, emigrated to America. (-3)
Mr. and Mrs. Lehmann Fleischhacker settled in Palestine. (-2)
Mr. Carl Ehmann left for the U.S.A. (-1)

May 24. Performances of a film about Palestine, *Promised Land*, in the large room of the White Dove. Two showings were filled to capacity with a local audience as well as visitors.
Mr. Fritz Stein and Dr. Hans Capell, Nuremberg, made the introductions. To everybody's pleasant surprise, business at the White Dove is picking up steadily. Many out-of-towners visit the restaurant, especially on Sundays.

June 2. Died: Mr. Bernhard Hecht. [-1]

June 2. Get-together in the W[hite] D[ove]. Mr. Fritz Stein and Mr. Julius Strauss talked about their trips to Palestine.

June 7. Wedding in Munich of Mr. Stefan Rossheimer and Miss Erna Marx, of Munich. (+1)

June 19. Died: Mr. Rudolf Fleischmann, 47, after a long illness. (-1)

June 21. Mr. and Mrs. Adolf Marx moved to Berlin. (-2)
The Oskar Marx family emigrated to America. (-2)

The following recently left Bamberg: Rudolf Treumann (Holland), Ernst Fein, Willy Schütz, (London), Lisa Silbermann, Rudolf Holzinger. (-5)

June 20. Arrival: Mr. Kahn, father-in-law of Mr. Gustav Fleischmann, from Koblenz. (+1)

Aug. 5. Died: Mr. Julius Abraham, 63. (-1); Mr. Max Reinhold. (-1)

Aug. 10. By ministerial ordinance all Jewish religious instruction in Bavarian schools is suspended.
Arrival: Isner family from Burghaslach. (+3)

Aug. 16. Wedding of Mr. Kurt Kleestadt and Miss Martha Neumann, Bamberg. The couple will live in Reutlingen. (-2)
Mr. Siegfried Polatschek, Augsburg, was married to Miss Anny Hermann, Schesslitz. They will reside in Augsburg.
Wedding of Mr. Ludwig Männlein and Miss Eva Baumann. They will emigrate to Sweden. (-2)

Aug. 18. Died: Mrs. Lina Silbermann, née Steinheimer, 64.

Aug. 20. Departures: Hans Friedmann, Ludwig Goldschmidt. (-2)

Aug. 20. Arrivals: Reifenberger family, from Weilburg. (+2); Mrs. Marie Bickart, from Nuremberg. (+1)
Mr. Max Wiesenfelder married Miss Tilly Rehbock.

Sept. 2. Died: Counselor Julius Buxbaum, 59. (-1)
Mrs. Jakob Schmidt settled in Palestine to join her son. (-1)

Sept. 10. Mrs. Therese Strauss emigrated with her daughter and son-in-law. (-2)

Oct. 10. Sally Goldschmidt family emigrated to the U.S.A.(-3)

Joseph Wiesenfelder family emigrated to the U.S.A. (-3)

Oct. 25. Dr. Ernst Wachtel and family emigrated to Brazil (Sao Paulo). (-3)

Dir. Max Willstatter and family emigrated to Austria (Wiener Neustadt). (-4)

Dr. Kandel and family emigrated to the U.S.A. (-2)

Oct. 28. Died: Mrs. Sabine Feldmann, née Mund, 52. (-1)

Nov. 6. Special classes for Jewish children in the public elementary school system opened. Thirty-eight children are enrolled in 7 grades. Mr. Justin Fränkel, Erlangen, was appointed to the position of teacher. The government of Upper Franconia hired Mr. Fränkel under a contract without pension rights and dismissal on 4 months notice. The city pays the salary. The school premises are the former conference room in the synagogue. Fixtures are the property of the city.

Died: Mrs. Selma Lipp, 40, wife of Mr. Heinrich Lipp. (-1)

Rolf Kahn left for London. (-1)

Nov. 23. Moritz Goldschmidt family emigrated to the U.S.A. (-4); Katzenstein family emigrated to the U.S.A. (-2)

Nov. 25. Lecture by Dr. Eduard Strauss, Frankfurt. Topic: "Is There a Concept Called Judaism?"

Dec. 6. Gertrude Steinberger emigrated to the U.S.A. (-1)

Dec. 8. Died: Mr. Siegfried Freudenberger. (-1)

Dec. 13. Hanukkah party at the synagogue. Children's choir. Recitation: "The Miracle."

Dec. 16. An evening of humor with Dela Lipinskaja at the Culture Club.

Dec. 20. Mr. Ernst Fein emigrated to the U.S.A. (-1)

Population Statistics, End of 1936
Population end of 1935—795
Decrease: Death—17
Departures—56
Total—722
Increase: Birth—0
Arrival—12
Marriage—1
Total—735

1937

Jan. 10. H. Gumbert emigrated to North America. (-1)

Jan. 16. Died: Mr. Joseph Eschwege, after a long illness.

(-1)

Jan 15. Arrival: Frank family from Saalfeld. (+3)

Jan. 18. Died: Mrs. Sali Gerstner, 61. (-1)

Jan. 22. Eng. Ernst Haymann and wife moved to Bogota (Colombia). (-2)

Jan. 23. Mr. Leopold Hess died suddenly at the age of 73. (-1)

Jan. 23. Lecture by Dr. Ernst Lichtenstein at the Jewish Culture Club. Topic: "Modern Jewish Poetry." Recitations by Werner Buloofzer. Speaker and performer received great applause.

Jan. 24. Birth of a son to Felix Hahn, merchant, and his wife Anni Ullmann. (+1)

Jan. 27. Died: Widow Ida Oster, née Hommel, 72. (-1)

Feb. 7. Wedding of Siegbert Kahn, Sonneberg, and Miss Meta Strauss, Straubing.
Benefit performance for Winter Relief in the big hall at the White Dove. Participating performers: Miss Hede Kaufmann, Bayreuth, Cantor Scheuermann, and Mrs. Holt-Landecker, Hamburg.

Feb. 5. Wedding of Ernst Fein and Miss Hilde Fleissig, in London. They are on their way to the U.S.A.

Feb. 21. Evening of dance and calisthenics by the pupils of Dr. Annie Rauh's Gymnastic School at the White Dove. Proceeds benefited the Winter Relief.

Feb. 23. Cabaret Erlich, Berlin, under the direction of Claire Arnstein, at the Jewish Kulturbund.

Feb. 28. Minska (stateless) joined her mother in Paris. (-1)
Arrival: Widow Kahn from Gleicherwiesen. (+1)

March 24. Died: Mr. Aron Cysner, 73, a shoemaker and the last of the Jewish artisans in Bamberg.

Mar. 31. Died: Mrs. Babette Steinberger, 72, retired. (-1); Mr. Moritz Grausmann, 81. (-1)

Apr. 10. Mr. David Nussbaum and family moved to the U.S.A. (Brooklyn). (-3)
Emigrated to the U.S.A.: Miss Martha Sternberg (-1); Mr. Hugo Oppenheimer (to Brooklyn) (-1); Mr. Felix Hahn (to New York) (-1).

Apr. 15. Miss Martha Ehrlich moved to Florence (-1); Erwin Steinberger moved to Winterthur (Switzerland) (-1).

Apr. 25. Arrival: Lein family from Diespeck. (+3)

Apr. 15. Birth of a daughter, Liselotte, to Mr. Ludwig Gold-meier. (+1)
Departures: Miss Luise Silbermann, Hilde Lipp. (-2)

Apr. 28. A number of rooms on the upper floor of the White Dove were readied for the opening of a Hehalutz Heim [Pioneer Home]. There are accommodations for 12 halutzim.

May 15. The holy ark from the dismantled Buttenheim synagogue was installed in the vestibule of our synagogue. The ornamentation of the ark is an extremely beautiful sample of early rococo. Around 1800 a nondescript coat of paint was applied. The ark is now restored to its original colors, with a generous application of gold leaf. The ceiling vault of the former Horb synagogue is in the possession of the Bamberg municipality. The installation of this artifact in our vestibule would greatly enhance the display.

May 19. Wedding of Mr. Heinrich Lipp and Miss Hilde Reichmannsdorfer of Trabelsdorf. (+1)

May 25. Miss Amalie Friedmann married Chone Stern in Dresden. (-1)
A wedding canopy, donated to the synagogue in Bayersdorf in 1713 by Rabbi Moses Goldschmidt, was put into the custody of our community by the Union of Jewish Communities of Bavaria. It is now displayed in our synagogue.

May 21. Died: The widow Josefine Lewy, née Hermann. (-1)
Max Hirnheimer family moved to Berlin. (-3)

June 10. Anneliese Fleischmann emigrated to England. (-1)
Mr. and Mrs. Max Wachtel emigrated to San Francisco, U.S.A. (-2)

June 25. Wedding of Miss Edith Morgenroth and Arnold Meyer, Nordhausen. (-1)

July 18. Ruth Fleischmann moved to England. (-1)
Ludwig Willy Schütz married out of the faith. (-1)

July 21. Died: Mrs. Klara Schloss, wife of Mr. Luis Schloss, (-1).
Engagement in New York: Mr. Karl Kohn and Miss Martha Sternberg, formerly of Bamberg; also Mr. Justin Isner and Miss Lily Neumann, formerly of Bamberg.

Aug. 20. Miss Vera Morgenroth moved to London. (-1)
Moritz Weiss family moved to Vienna. (-4)
Mr. Luitpold Neumann married Miss Eva Lederer, both formerly of Bamberg.

Sept. 1. Dr. Lang and family emigrated. (-4)
Martin Adler emigrated to the U.S.A. (-1)
Martha Ehrlich returned to Bamberg. (+1)
Jakob Ansbacher, E. Aigner, Bleicher moved to Munich for further educational training (-3). Ilse Wiesenfeld emigrated to the U.S.A. (-1)
Mrs. Laura Mondschein returned to her home in Wiesenthal. (-1); her husband, Max Mondschein, died in a convalescent home in Würzburg.

Sept. 20. Died: Mr. Max Stein, 72, longtime treasurer of the community. (-1) Hans Treumann moved to London. (-1)

Sept. 22. Died: Mrs. Karoline Wald, 90. A devout and revered woman. (-1)

Sept. 30. Mrs. Ernestine Rokozinsky died at the old-age home at Würzburg. Burial was here. (-1)

Oct. 1. Miss Hanna Hirnheimer moved to Nuremberg. (-1)

Oct. 5. Died: Mrs. Hannchen Dessauer, 81. (-1)

Oct. 15. Cantor Lent and wife left the congregation to seek a new life in Argentina. The choir, the board of trustees, and the officers of the congregation met with the departing couple at a modest farewell dinner. Mr. Lent had held the position of cantor since 1926. (-2)

Oct. 15. George Palm moved to Frankfurt to join the orchestra of the Kulturbund. (-1)

Oct. 15. Kurt Kleestadt and wife returned to Bamberg. (+2) Mr. Adolf Forchheimer replaced Mr. Lent as sexton of the synagogue. He also took over the functions of the cemetery attendant, Mr. Nussbaum, who left Bamberg. (-1)

Oct. 31. Mrs. Hermine Ullmann died in Berlin. (-1)

Nov. 5. Died: Counselor Paul Awrach, an outstanding jurist and active person. (-1)
Mr. Ludwig Goldschmidt, Kurt Baum emigrated to the U.S.A. (-2)

Dec. 1. Berthold Katz family moved to Berlin. (-4)

Dec. 15. Miss Milka Weil emigrated to the U.S.A. (-1)

Dec. 10. Wedding of Miss Friedel Fleischmann in Frankfurt. (-1)

Dec. 17. Died: Mr. Max Spier, 71. (-1)
Arrival: Miss Martha Vollweiler. (+1)
In a civil ceremony Mr. Emil Palm married divorcee Emily Ansbacher. (+1)

Membership of the congregation, beginning of 1937—735
Decrease: Death—17

Marriage to out-of-town partners—4
Departures: 43[3]
Total—671
Increase: Arrival—12
Birth—2
Total as of Jan. 1, 1938—685

1938

Jan. 1. Mr. and Mrs. Kurt Kleestadt moved to Lübeck. (-2)
Arrival: Teacher Paul Possenheimer. (+1)
Emigrated to the U.S.A.: Mrs. Anni Hahn and son Michael
(-2), and Mrs. Friedl Sacki. (-1)
Arrival: Mrs. Schwed. (+1)
Addendum: Mr. Abraham Kohn moved to the old-age home
in Fürth. (-1)

Jan. 2. Died: Mr. Gustav Kahn, 66. (-1)

Jan. 2. Mariechen Kohn, Sepp Kohn, engaged to be married,
emigrated to the U.S.A. (-2)

Jan. 5. Died: Mr. Max Reichmann, 86. Burial was in Fürth. (-
1). Mr. Paul Possenheimer, the new teacher, will be in charge of
the segregated classes for Jewish children. He also will conduct
services on weekdays.
Ernst Simon moved to Berlin, to be apprenticed to a tailor. (-
1)

Jan. 10. Mr. Sonnenfeld moved to Berlin. (-1)

Jan. 17. Birth of a son, Michael, to Mr. Fritz Stein and his
wife Bella, née Dittmann. (+1)

---

3 The German text lists 73 people in this category, apparently a typo-
graphical error.

Lecture classes instituted by Dr. Edward Strauss, Frankfurt, attracted many participants.

Jan. 16. Miss Kessel, Hamburg, will teach gymnastics to the girls in the Jewish school. She will be available for private lessons for women and children. (+1)

Walter Fleischmann emigrated to the U.S.A. (-1)

Feb. 10. Departures: Miss Dora Fleischhacker (-1), Reifenberg family and Benno Hessberg family (-3), Lieben family (-2).

Died: Mrs. Sidonie Saalheimer, 78. (-1)

Feb. 7. Birth of a daughter, Gabriela Judith, to Mr. Stefan Rossheimer and his wife Erna, née Marx. (+1)

Feb. 20. Attorney Ludwig Löw and family moved to New York. (-4)

Feb. 26. Herbert Dames left for Palestine with a youth group. (-1)

Mar. 20. Aron Hahn family emigrated to the U.S.A. (-2)

Mar. 10. Martin Hahn emigrated to Czechoslovakia. (-1)

Otto Rosenblüth and wife moved away. (-2)

Mar. 16. Joseph Singer emigrated to Palestine. (-1)

Mar. 17. Died: Mrs. Sophie Kohn, née Reichmannsdorfer. (-1)

Mar. 18. Died: Mrs. Marie Baum, née Krauss. (-1)

Mar. 20. Mr. Kurt Wollenberg emigrated to the U.S.A. (-1)

Mar. 21. Wedding of Herbert Ackermann and Miss Brunhilde Luchs, Buttenwiesen.

Mar. 24. Mrs. Clara Lessing, at the age of 78. (-1)

Mar. 27. Mrs. Jettchen Spier moved to Berlin; her daughter Ida to Kiel. (-2)
Arrival: Sacki family from Berburg. (+2)
Siegfried Simon family moved to Berlin. (-4)

Mar. 29. Died: Mrs. Siegmunde Kronacher, née Lehmann, 80.(-1)

Apr. 1. Hans Kohn emigrated to the U.S.A. (-1)

Apr. 3. Berthold Kahn family emigrated to Argentina. (-2)

Apr. 5. Pharmacist Dr. Otto Holzinger emigrated to Switzerland. (-2)

Apr. 27. Wedding: Mr. Hans Frank and Dr. Olga Buchsbaum. (-1)
Thea Saalheimer, Ruth Kalischak moved to Berlin. (-2)
H. Awrach moved to Munich (apprenticeship). (-1)

Apr. 28. Mr. Abraham Kohn, 85, died at the hospital in Fürth. He was a longtime member of the community's executive committee. He also led the weekday services.

May 1. Arrival: Siegm. Rosenbacher family from Ebelsbach. (+3)

May 8. Birth of a son, Tom Michael, to Mr. Erich Jacobsohn and his wife Grete, née Simon. (+1)
Arrivals: Nathan Fleischmann family from Ebelsbach (+3); Mr. Guthmann, father-in-law of Leo Sacki (+1).

May 20. Mrs. Frieda Ullmann emigrated to the U.S.A. (-1)

May 29. Died: Mrs. Line Frank, 72. (-1)

June 10. Emigrated to the U.S.A.: Mr. Herbert Eschwege (-1) and Mr. Weinheimer (-1).

July 17. Died: Mr. Karl Wassermann, 64. (-1)

Aug. 5. Died: Mr. Hermann Fleischmann, 88. (-1)

Aug. 17. Died: Mr. Louis Schloss, 72 (-1); Mrs. Sofie Klestadt (-1).

Sept. 3. Mr. Fritz Stein emigrated to Palestine. (-3)

Sept. 8. Mrs. Else Treumann emigrated to the U.S.A. (-2)

Sept. 10. Emigrated to Palestine: Hans Kurt Fleischmann (-1) and Miss Judith Schapiro (-1).

Aug. Birth of a daughter, Lea Judith, to Ignatz Prager, merchant, and his wife Frieda, née Naumann, temporarily residing in Bamberg.

Aug. Arrival: Mr. and Mrs. Justin Baumann. (+2)

Aug. Miss Kessel moved to Hamburg. (-1)

Sept. 4. Wedding of Mr. Paul Pretzfelder and Miss Margot Sternglanz.
Kurt Kleestadt and wife returned to Bamberg. (+2)

Aug. Family Ernst Stein emigrated to Switzerland. (-3)

Sept. Counselor Löw and wife emigrated to Palestine. (-2]

Sept. Emigrated to the U.S.A.: Goldmeier family (-3); Sternberg family (-3); Dr. Karl Rauh family (-3).

Sept. Arrival: Mrs. Engelmann, née Sack. (+1]

Oct. 3. Died: Mrs. Julie Bechmann, née Sulzbacher, 76. (-1)

Addendum: Max Wiesenfelder family moved to Frankfurt/ Main. (-2)

Oct. 20. Dentist Dr. Bähr emigrated to the U.S.A. (-3)
Miss Klärchen Herschtal emigrated to the U.S.A. (-1)

Oct. 31. Mrs. Jette Lipp, née Bloch, died while visiting her daughter in Kassel. (-1)

Appendix 2

Time schedule of Jewish elementary school in Bamberg (Nov. 5, 1936 to Mar. 30 1937)

Hour	Grade	Monday	Tuesday	Wednesday	Thursday	Friday	Saturday
8-9	1	—	—		—	—	—
	2 & 3	Arithmetic	Religion		Religion	Arithmetic	
	4 & 5	Religion	Arithmetic	Arithmetic	Arithmetic	Religion	
	7 & 8	Arithmetic				Arithmetic	
9-10	1	Arithmetic	Religion	Arithmetic	Religion	Arithmetic	
	2 & 3	Religion	Arithmetic	Writing/Reading	Arithmetic	Writing/Reading	
	4 & 5	Arithmetic	Reading	Natural Science	Grammar	Arithmetic	
	7 & 8	Grammar				Grammar	
10-11	1	Religion	Writing	Music	Reading/Writing	Music	
	2 & 3	Reading	Reading	Grammar	Grammar		
	4 & 5	Spelling	Grammar	Religion		Grammar	
	7 & 8			Grammar	Geography	History	
	1	—	—	—	—	—	
	2 & 3	Grammar	Grammar			Grammar	
	4 & 5	Reading	Composition	Music	Reading/Writing		
	7 & 8	Religion			Grammar	Composition	
2-3	1	Reading/Writing	Music		Local History		
	2 & 3	Calligraphy	Local History		Geography	Choir	
	4 & 5	Reading &	Spelling				
	7 & 8	Grammar			Religion	—	
3-4	1		Drawing				
	2 & 3						
	4 & 5	Gymnastics	History	—	Gymnastics		
	7 & 8		Religion	—			

1. Religion: identify lessons given by clergy, e.g. ("Religion [Evangelical]").
Also list religious instruction given by minority faiths.
2. List trade school courses.

Summary of Lessons

1.	Religion	4 hrs.
2.	German	7 hrs.
3.	Music[1]	2 hrs.
4.	Local History	1 hrs.
5.	Geography	1 hrs.
6.	History	1 hrs.
7.	Natural Science	1 hrs.
8.	Arithmetic	6 hrs.
9.	Drawing	1 hrs.
10.	Gymnastics	2 hrs.
11.	Domestic Science for girls	2 hrs.

Summary of hours taught

a) elementary 26

b) Advanced elementary

Appendix 3

Pictures turned over to the Bamberg Finance Department for eventual sale (Sept. 18, 1943)

Jd. No.	Former owner	Description	Value (in reichmarks)
738/39	Lessing Otto, Hain St. 7	Simon and Pero	200.-
738/39	Lessing Otto, Hain St. 7	Still Life	200.-
908	Ludwig or Curt Mosbacher, Friedrich St. 7	Impression of Thunderstorm	500.-
739/39	Lessing Otto, Hain St. 7	Tavern (on wood)	40.-
163/65	Else Wassermann, Schützen St. 1	City Scene	20.-
741	Hugo Marx, Franz-Ludwig St. 26	Sleigh Ride	10.-
741	Hugo Marx, Franz-Ludwig St. 26	Sleigh Ride	30.-
163/65	Else Wassermann, Schützen St. 21	Ruins in Tivoli	8.-
73/74	Oskar Fleischmann, Kunigundendamm 1	Nude	10.-
163/65	Else Wassermann, Schützen St. 21	Venice	20.-
163/65	Else Wassermann, Schützen St. 21	Venice	20.-
73/74	Oskar Fleischmann, Kunigundendamm 1	Japanese Painting	3.-
163/65	Else Wassermann, Schützen St. 21	Park at the Palace	10.-
73/740	Oskar Fleischmann, Kunigundendamm 1	Devil and Tailor	2.-
1163/65	Else Wassermann, Schützen St. 21	Courtyard at the Castle	.50

16	717	Becker, Nathan, Zinkenwörth 17	Portrait of Church Dignitary	150.-
17	741	Hugo Marx, Franz-Ludwig St. 26	Oriental Painting	5.-
18	741	Hugo Marx, Franz-Ludwig St. 26	Hermit	20.-
19	163/65	Else Wassermann, Schützen St. 21	Winter Scene	1.-
20	133	Martha Morgenroth, Sofien St. 12	Horse Market	.50
21	163/65	Else Wassermann, Schützen St. 21	Citadel at Montefort	.50
22	102	Josef Hessberg, Friedrich St. 7	Avenue of Poplars	-.50
23	163/65	Else Wassermann, Schützen St. 21	Chicks	-.50
24		Else Wassermann, Schützen St. 21	Scenes	3.-
25		Else Wassermann, Schützen St. 21	Scenes	3.-
26		Else Wassermann,Schützen St. 21	Temple	2.-
27		Else Wassermann, Schützen St. 21	View of Wallerstein	1.-
28	73/74	Oskar Fleischmann, Kunigundendamm 1	Venice	2.-
29	163/65	Else Wassermann, Schützen St. 21	Village Scene	-.80
30		Else Wassermann, Schützen St. 21	Portrait	1.-
31	67	Greti Feith, Friedrich St. 7	Tapestry	5.-
32	67	Greti Feith, Friedrich St. 7	Tapestry	5.-
33	67	Greti Feith, Friedrich St. 7	Tapestry	5.-
34	738/39	Lessing Otto, Hain Str. 7	Portrait of Woman	20.-
35		Lessing Otto, Hain Str. 7	Color Print	10.-
36		Lessing Otto, Hain Str. 7	Color Print	10.-
37		Lessing Otto, Hain Str. 7	Family in Garden	8.-
38		Lessing Otto, Hain Str. 7	Portrait	5.-
39		Lessing Otto, Hain Str. 7	Portrait	10.-
40		Lessing Otto, Hain Str. 7	"Portrait	5.-
41	163/65	Else Wassermann, Schützen St. 21	Needlepoint	3.-
42		Else Wassermann, Schützen St. 21	Portrait	20.-
43	104	Leopold Hessberg, Franz-Ludwig St. 26	Dutch Woman	10.-

44	102	Josef Hessberg, Friedrich St. 7	The Sick Town Councillor	1.-
45	738/39	Lessing Otto, Hain St. 7	Flower Vendor	1.50
46	163/65	Else Wassermann, Schützen St. 21	Portrait (no value)	-.-
47		Else Wassermann, Schützen St. 21	Portrait	35.-
48	137	Max Pretzfelder, Hain St. 4a	Hunt Scene	2.-
49	163/65	Else Wassermann, Schützen St. 21	Portrait	10.-
50	738/39	Lessing Otto, Hain St. 7	The Dragon Rock	10.-
51	137	Max Pretzfelder, Hain St.4a	5 pictures:Joseph's Brothers	200.-
52	73/74	Oskar Fleischmann, Heinrichsdamm 1	Flutist	50.-
53	738/39	Lessing Otto, Hain St. 7	Portrait	20.-
54		Lessing Otto, Hain St. 7	Still Life	50.-
55		Lessing Otto, Hain St. 7	Portrait (no value)	-.-
56		Lessing Otto, Hain St. 7	Portrait	5.-
57		Lessing Otto, Hain St. 7	Portrait	10.-
58	104	Leopold Hessberg, Franz-Ludwig St. 7	Bedouin	5.-
59	137	Max Pretzfelder, Hain St. 4a	Harbor	2.-
60	163/65	Else Wassermann, Schützen St. 21	On the Beach	1.-
61	154	Rositta Silbermann, Luitpold St. 48	Sailing Party	30.-
62	765/IV	Elise Neisser, Lagarde St. 41	Portrait	5.-
63		Elise Neisser, Lagarde St. 41	Christmas Presents	1.-
64	738	Lessing Otto, Hain St.	73 pictures: "Japanese Paintings"	1.50
65	63/65	Else Wassermann, Schützen St. 21	Tavern	1.-
66	104	Leopold Hessberg, Franz-Ludwig St. 26	Castle	2.-
67	163/65	Else Wassermann, Schützen St. 21	Harbor	1.-
68	738/39	Lessing Otto, Hain St. 7	Quartet	10.-
69	104	Leopold Hessberg, Franz-Ludwig St. 26	Schiller in Stuttgart	2.-

70	104	Leopold Hessberg, Franz-Ludwig St. 26	Under Flowering Trees	1.-
71	152	Rositta Silbermann, Luitpold St. 48	Party in the Woods	4.-
72	906	Ludwig or Curt Mosbacher, Friedrich St. 7	Portrait	50.-
73	162/65	Else Wassermann, Schützen St. 21	Bamberg Cathedral (damaged)	.50
74	738/39	Lessing Otto, Hain St. 7	Gries of London	5.-
75	133	Marta Morgenroth, Sofien St. 12	Joseph's Brothers	60.-
76	738	Lessing Otto, Hain St. 7	Portrait	2.-
77	63/64	Jakob Dessauer, Schillerplatz 18	Mountain Brook	150.-
78	133	Martha Morgenroth, Sofien St. 12	Horse Race	200.-
79	104	Leopold Hessberg, Franz-Ludwig St. 26	Oriental Scene (damaged)	-.-
80	163/65	Else Wassermann, Schützen St. 21	Study	-.50
81	163/65	Else Wassermann, Schützen St. 21	Chapel	-.50
82	738/39	Lessing Otto, Hain St. 7	Officers	50.-
83	83	Tina Frank, Franz-Ludwig St. 26	Sheep Pen	200.-
84	83	Tina Frank, Franz-Ludwig St. 26	Sheep Pen	200.-
85	157	Albert Walter, Sofien St. 7	Party in the Woods	200.-
87	163/65	Else Wassermann, Schützen St. 21	Ruins	3.-
88	715/58	Dr. Bauchwitz, Hain St. 7	Nuremberg	5.-
89	715/56	Dr. Bauchwitz, Hain St. 7	Country Road	5.-
90	715	Dr. Bauchwitz, Hain St. 7	Still Life	50.-
91	741	Hugo Marx, Franz-Ludwig St. 26	Warrior	25.-
92	715	Dr. Bauchwitz, Hain St. 7	Still Life	50.-
93	163/65	Else Wassermann, Schützen St. 21	Harbor Party	300.-
94	906	Ludwig or Curt Mosbacher, Friedrich St. 7	Dutch Winter Scene	150.-
95	906	Ludwig or Curt Mosbacher, Friedrich St. 7	Rider	100.-
96	715	Dr. Bauchwitz, Hain St. 7	5 Miniatures @ 20.-	100.-

97	738/39	Lessing Otto, Hain St. 7	Cellist	50.-
98	IV/715/154	Dr. Bauchwitz, Hain St. 7	Le Billet doux	10.-
99	IV715/33	Dr. Bauchwitz, Hain St. 7	Portrait	20.-
100	IV715/33	Dr. Bauchwitz, Hain St. 7	Portrait	20.-
101	IV 765	Elise Neisser, Lagarde St. 41	Smithy	20.-
102	IV 765	Elise Neisser, Lagarde St. 41	Tailor Shop	5.-
103	IV 765	Elise Neisser, Lagarde St. 41	Hamburg	10.-
104	IV 765	Elise Neisser, Lagarde St. 41	4 Color Prints	10.-
105	IV 765	Elise Neisser, Lagarde St. 41	Needlepoint	10.-
106	IV 765	Elise Neisser, Lagarde St. 41	Coachman	10.-
107	IV 765	Elise Neisser, Lagarde St. 41	Charlottenbrunn	5.-
108	IV 765	Elise Neisser, Lagarde St. 41	Sutler	5.-
109	IV 765	Elise Neisser, Lagarde St. 41	Marsh	3.-
110	IV 765	Elise Neisser, Lagarde St. 41	Beadwork	3.-
111	IV 715/155	Dr. Bauchwitz, Hain St. 7	Gries of London	10.-
112	IV 765	Elise Neisser, Lagarde St. 41	Color Portrait	10.-
113	IV 765	Elise Neisser, Lagarde St. 41	Portrait Sketch	2.-
114	IV 715	Dr. Bauchwitz, Hain St. 7	Landscape	5.-
115	IV 715	Dr. Bauchwitz, Hain St. 7	1 Ink Drawing (Nursing Mother)	5.-
116	IV 715	Dr. Bauchwitz, Hain St. 71	1 Small Engraving (Chapel of St. Ann)	2.50
117	IV 765	Elise Neisser, Lagarde St. 41	1 Small Color Print (Erdmannsdorf)	2.50
118	IV 765	Elise Neisser, Lagarde St. 41	1 Small Color Print (Mountain Inn)	2.50
119	IV 765	Elise Neisser, Lagarde St. 41	1 Small Color Print (Hilltop Chapel & Inn)	2.50
120	IV 765	Elise Neisser, Lagarde St. 41	2 Large Family Portraits in color	10.-
			Reichmarks	3981.30